JUDY AND ME

Growing up in North Sydney, Cape Breton Island, God's Country, Nova Scotia in the 1950s.

What a Memory!!

ALLIE JEAN HODDER 1941 - 2010

ISBN: paperback book 978-1-987813-35-7

eBook 978-1-987813-36-4

PREVIOUS ISBN: 0-9684654-1-2 Ancaster Printing, 2004, 2007

Cover Image: Allie Jean Hodder(left), Judy Clark (right), Norma Jean (back)

Printed and distributed by Amazon and Kindle Direct Publishing, a division of Amazon.com

CONTENTS

This book is dedicated to our mom, Alice, a Bluenoser through and through. ***Judy and Me*** has been published to give it, and her, the hoopla they always deserved.

Fare thee well, mom.

Behind all your stories is always your mother's story.
Because hers is where yours begin.
~ Mitch Albom

Foreword

Judy and Me is my mother, Alice (Hodder Hoyt) Garland's memoir. Alice was born on May 12, 1941 in Halifax, Nova Scotia. She and her family moved to Cape Breton when her father, Rev. H.G. Hodder was assigned to a parish in Port Morien, Nova Scotia. Mom's memoir portrays her youth from the time she was eight years old, the day she moved to her beloved North Sydney, Cape Breton and met Judy Clark, who would become her lifelong best friend. After her mother, Blanche Garland, died in 1957 at the age of 37, Alice and her family moved to Halifax, leaving her friends and the memories of her mother behind. She longed for Cape Breton for the rest of her days.

When mom told my sisters, my brother and me that she was writing a memoir, we may not have given it, or her, the recognition they deserved. Her dear friend, Andy, helped her to compile her vignettes into a book. She printed the first edition of ***Judy and Me*** in 2004, reprinted in 2007, and distributed copies to family and friends. Most of us put it away with every intention of reading it one day. To be honest, I was a little miffed to see that I was not mentioned in her memoir. With one exception, the stories end just before I, the eldest of her four children, was born in 1961.

Having had time to re-read and re-type ***Judy and Me,*** and to reflect on my mom's youth, I can appreciate what a special time this had been for her. She would escape from the rectory and play records at Judy's house, dancing with Judy's brother, Donnie, and baby sister, Norma Jean. They were excited to hear a new talent, her beloved Elvis, who "shook" when he sang. She and her friends dated, danced and drank milkshakes at Josie's Diner.

Mom included pages of what she referred to as "lingo" at the end of the book. She would direct attention to this section that appeared to be a stream of consciousness. I contemplated omitting this section as it wasn't "writing," in my opinion. But perhaps these were stories she meant to tell. She had so much more to say.

The photos we have of Alice capture her physical beauty, "five foot two, eyes of blue" she would point out to us. Pictures tell a story but don't reveal a soul like stories do. Mom has passed the torch to my sisters and me, as we write our own stories. My adult children may be disappointed to know they aren't within these pages. Mom might have said, "They can write their own books, dear."

Mom died unexpectedly in 2010. We took her home to her beloved North Sydney and laid her to rest in the family plot beside her parents, her grandparents and her dog, Jessie. This trip became a family reunion, with some guests young enough to never have had the honour of meeting her in person.

The guest of honour, Judy, attended Mom's celebration of life. We ate finger sandwiches and date squares in the parish hall of St. John's Anglican Church, read excerpts from her memoir and met some of her friends from the soda shop. We toasted her memory. A slide show began with photos of her as a young child, and she grew before our eyes into a teen, a mother, and a granny to ten "beauties." Her dimples were evident in each snap accompanied by the songs, "Can't Take My Eyes Off of You" (Frankie Valli) and "Fare Thee Well Love" (The Rankins). I have included my eulogy to mom in this publication, as I believe it captures the essence of her.

Born Alice Jean Hodder, the author was known as Allie Jean in her youth. She married in 1961 and assumed the surname, Hoyt. She legally changed her surname to Garland, in honour of her maternal ancestors, after she launched her adult children. Other monikers were Mom, Granny and Alicia. Her children knew her as "Mom," although she always signed off her frequent correspondence as "Mum." Everyone referred to her as fun, loyal and loving. She referred to herself as "a people person," who was a wonderful judge of character. She wasn't wrong.

In her life, mom was held and cared for by her beloved maternal grandmother, Alice Garland, who was born in 1887. And Mom cuddled her own baby grandchildren whose children I hope to meet one day. Her grandchildren were her pride and joy. I hope that members of the next Hodder-Garland generation will read ***Judy and Me*** to enjoy stories that otherwise would go untold about their Maritime ancestors. Perhaps they will write their own stories.

Without further ado, may I introduce ***Judy and Me.*** Only minor edits have been made to the original manuscript. Her jargon, literary style and prolific punctuation have been preserved.
Enjoy!

Allison (Hoyt) Hannah
July 2020

I didn't lose my mother when she died. I found her.
~Jann Arden

Judy and Me

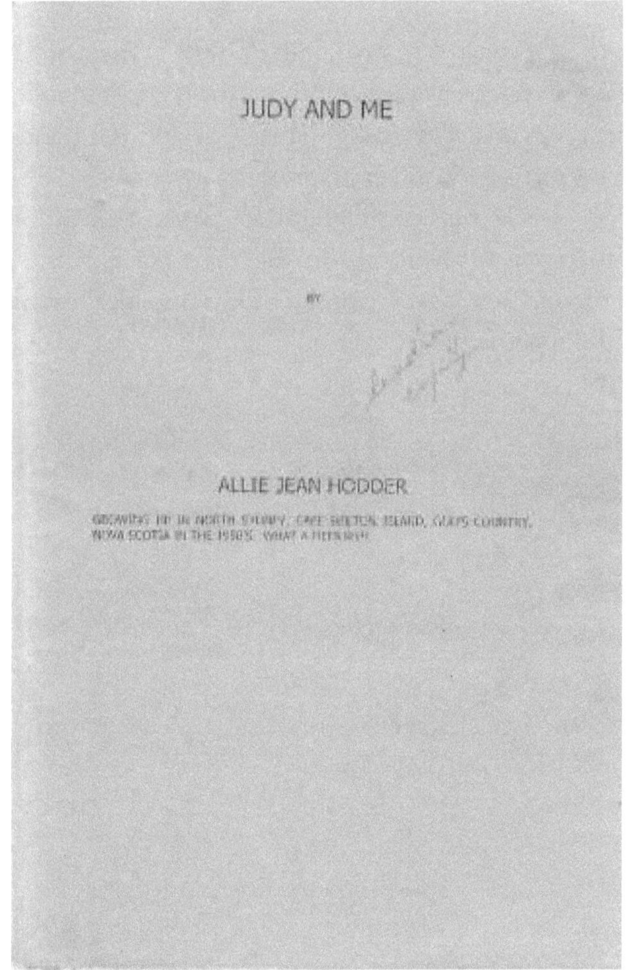

JUDY AND ME

BY

ALLIE JEAN HODDER

Judy and Me. First Printing 2004. Lending Copy

The Author's Dedication

This book is dedicated to my family and many friends, "upstairs and downstairs" who have always been there for me in thought, word and deed. Sherry, Virginia, "mother", Janis, Uli, and Andy and so many others. What can I say? Forever grateful.

I had so much fun compiling this book. So many wonderful memories to recall. Growing up in the right place at the right time. "northside friends" are "forever friends." I had no idea how many things Judy and I did together. We never quit!

With love,
Alicia
AJH

The Vignettes

Meeting Judy

Judy and I met when we were eight years old. I am one month and six days older. It was our moving day to North Sydney, Cape Breton Island, Nova Scotia. God's country! We came from Port Morien, not too far away, to St. John's Church, North Sydney, my father's new church. He is a Church of England Minister.

Mary came with us. Mary is from Little Bay, Newfoundland. She left her home and family and came to help us all out in Port Morien. Mary was my mother's helper with the housework and helped mind us kids. She scrubbed the floors, made and changed our beds. Mary vacuumed all the rooms, swept the kitchen and front hallway floor and the veranda. Mary also helped Mummy wash the clothes. She didn't mind doing any of it, at all, at all! Mary never ever complained.

Mary didn't marry and we were like her own kids. She was afraid of coal stoves because her father and brother died in a house fire years before. She always had her Evening of Paris cologne and talc powder on her dressing table with mirrors on the sides. My younger sister, Shirley and I could try them on when she invited us into her room. Mary would get letters from her family quite often and she would always answer right back. Mary's bedroom was always located at the top of the back stairs. She would invite us into her room quite often and we also got to look at her photo albums.

Mary's bedroom was handy for her to get to the kitchen in the mornings. She always went to church on Sunday. That was Mary's day off. That is the day when she would visit her friends. Ramsay would come and visit quite often during the week at our house. He always had a cigarette butt in the corner of his mouth. The tiniest butt you ever did see! He never burned himself at all and we were amazed he didn't! Ramsay had a strong Newfoundland accent. He was a very nice man and very comical.

Mary would go back to Little Bay to see her relatives for the month of July when we were on our holidays. She was very kind to my sister, Shirley and me. I could give her quite a bad time sometimes, but it was quickly forgotten. It was Tommy Arthur, my brother, who was Mary's favourite. Tommy Arthur could do no wrong with Mary or my Mummy. Mary bought him a black harness racing horse one birthday. He could sit in it and pedal it with his feet. Did he go! I think Mary ordered it from the Simpsons catalogue. What a surprise it was for Tommy Arthur! For all of us. It was such a beautiful gift. Mary was so pleased that he liked it! As our things and furniture were being moved into the rectory, I went outside to explore the front and side veranda and the yard. Judy was across the street standing by her front gate. She was wearing a two-piece top and shorts set and her hair in braids. She asked me if I was going to live here (pointing to our house). I said, "yes." We were both very happy to have found a friend. Me especially, just moving to a new place. We became fast friends. Judy was my mother's favourite. All of these days later, Judy is still my friend!

The Rectory

The Hodder family. Blanche holding Tommy Arthur, Rev. Hayward Hodder, Shirley (centre), Allie Jean (right)

The rectory, my house, was on King Street. Beside it was the parish hall and next to it, the church. Our house and buildings were all very distinctive, painted black with white trim. A black fence all around the front and side of the house. All three buildings took up the whole block. Maple trees lined the front yard and the Pierce Street side of the street. When Shirley and I were in her bedroom at night, we could look down on the sidewalk with no one knowing we were there. The tree leaves hiding us. It was very quiet and dark up there as we looked down. There was always someone coming and going to the parish hall or the church. Sometimes, we might see a boy and girl kissing! They would be coming from an A.Y. meeting and maybe heading for a car. We giggled at that.

There were two sets of stairs in our house. One set in the front hall and another leading up from the kitchen. We were always sliding down the banister on the front stairs. Much like a slide to be played on outside. Something you weren't supposed to be doing. Dangerous! We hid in the enclosed one. A good place for hide and seek. It was a great pastime. I spent a lot of time at my father's desk in the study. It was his work place. People would come to see him for any variety of reasons. I didn't know why, except if it was a wedding couple preparing for their marriage.

Daddy would also do his praying and reading in the study. The Gestetner copier by the far wall to print out the Sunday bulletins. One of the church ladies would type up the stencil. Shirley and I took turns helping daddy roll out the bulletins on Saturday night before the Sunday service. Our arms would get tired with all the handle turnings. There was a big desk in my daddy's study. The desk had a top drawer across the top and three drawers on each side. A swivel chair. A drawer full of white paper, envelopes, elastic bands and paper clips galore. Lots of pens and pencils. Two nibbed pens in a pen stand with two inkwells. Stamp pads, bottles of ink and church stampers. When you pulled down on the handles they would make an imprint with the church's name on the paper. It was fun using them. My papers looked very important with the seal at the top of the pages. I also liked to play bank. Making up my cheques and filling them out to myself. There was always change in the top drawer and I would count it out and put it into piles.

The black telephone was on daddy's desk. You could call someone in private in the study. No one knowing you were on the phone with the door closed. There was an upstairs telephone too, in mummy and daddy's bedroom. It was handy when Judy came over and we could both listen in to a call.

Our living room was across from the study. The living room had two sets of windows. One facing King Street and the other Pierce Street. We lived right on the corner. A white mantelpiece. A green chesterfield and chair. Two upholstered chairs, one maroon and the other cream with chrome arms. Mummy's piano, by the window, we all shared. The television set made the living room complete. Our bedrooms and the bathroom upstairs. There was another staircase up there leading to the spooky attic. Shirley and I didn't go up there and Tommy Arthur was too little.

There was always a flurry in the spring, "spring cleaning." The furniture in the living room and dining room would be moved into the centre of the rooms. A man would come and do the painting and the papering. He brought his ladder with him. He would put thick paste on each piece of wallpaper and then smooth it on evenly with a smoother. Putting up the wallpaper strips one by one. The lace curtains were washed and starched. The curtains would be put on frames and tacked down so they didn't shrink. It looked like we had a new house when it was all done. A wonderful smell all through the house!

The bathroom was the place for the bath. We had to be careful about using too much hot water as it didn't take too long before it turned cold. Familiar shouts from my daddy were, "turn off the water," "you are using too much water!" It was a quick bath as not too much water was covering you. It was no surprise to have a bath with your sister sitting behind you. To save on the water output. Stepping out of the tub or out of your bed in the morning was no picnic. Hardwood floors with only a few mats covering them. The floors would be so cold. You would be shivering. The house was heated by a coal furnace. The man would come with his truck full of coal. He would open the trap door to the basement and shovel it all in. Daddy would keep the furnace going until bedtime. He would be down in the basement the first thing in the morning, stoking it up so we would be warm. At Christmas time we were in fear we would get a piece of coal in our stockings. If you weren't good! A dreaded thing!

Music

We played "Chopsticks" on our piano. Banging on the keys was another thing to be doing. We would also play by ear. Daddy would be shushing us and telling us to give it up as it got on his nerves. "Stop the racket." Daddy would want us to learn to play, but he didn't want to hear it! Many times, my mummy took the time to teach us a piece. "Silver

Bells," "Unchained Melody," and "When He Cometh" come to mind. Mummy is an excellent piano player and sometimes plays in the Sunday school.

Mummy also teaches Sunday school. I took piano lessons from Professor Briers later on. I didn't like the practicing and the serious lessons, really having to concentrate on it hard. Doing the scales over and over without getting my fingers tripped up. My head would be in a tizzy. I couldn't wait for the lesson to be over. It was more fun playing on your own. You had to curl up your fingers when you played for Professor Briers or he would tap his ruler over your knuckles. It didn't hurt too much, but you were embarrassed and didn't feel like playing anymore. He and Mrs. Briers have two daughters, Alyce and Jean. They lived in Sydney Mines.

Playing Outdoors

Judy and I occupied our time that summer and others after, playing hop scotch. We got our long pieces of chalk from my father's study drawer. We made our squares on the sidewalk. We would throw in our rock and hop and top trying to keep our balance. We would also wheel around on our roller skates. We fell down so many times scraping our knees. Sometimes, one or two skates would fall off. We always had our keys handy to tighten them up around our shoes. We felt very grown up when we graduated to our two wheeled bicycles. What a thrill that was! The wind whipping through our hair. Whizzing through the neighbourhood streets! The speed of it all! We didn't go down on Commercial Street because of the cars. It was much too busy down there. It was much busier than our street, King Street.

Playing in the Church

Judy and I spent so much time at the parish hall and the church. Because that was where mostly everything was happening. Judy belonged to the United Church but spent double time at mine. We had Junior Auxiliary, Girls Auxiliary, AYPA, choir, and church attendance four times on a Sunday and Sunday school. The Boy Scouts, the Girl Guides, the Cubs and the Brownies also had their meetings in the parish hall. The Dominion Drama Festival began shortly after we moved to North Sydney, so we had the opportunity of seeing plays and some of us acting in them. Each Church of England was represented. The actors performed at each other's parish halls. Sometimes, you might see four or five plays in an evening. I loved it! Bob Patey and I got to be in one, one year, acting as boyfriend and girlfriend. Flo got us interested. I was a bit nervous at first but soon I really liked it. Hannah Pye from Sydney Mines won for best actress. I got an honourable mention. Mr. Major, the adjudicator, didn't like the way I said "house" and "mouse" with my Cape Breton accent! The comedienne, Toots Rowe Hart, came to entertain, and Hughie and Allan one time. Toots did great comedy skits about baseball games and baseball players. One year, I missed them because I got the red measles and I had to stay in bed. I wasn't allowed to go near anyone. I wasn't too happy about having to stay home. Whatever was going on, Judy and I were there.

Our favourite places were the parish hall and the church to play in. We would go up on the church balcony and look down over the seats. Singing in our loudest voices for an echo effect. We got a little dizzy but we were always careful about not falling over. The pews were also a favourite hiding place. Playing under them. Crawling around all over the floor so we couldn't find each other. No one else could find us either. Then, we would head for the pulpit and preach our individual sermons really loudly. Then, on to the wonderful pipe organ, lifting the lid very carefully and turning on the button. We played the two keyboards, pulled the stops out and used the foot pedals. The many pipe organ pipes behind us. We made some wonderful sounds. Music? To our ears anyway. We always thought no one was the wiser about our using it, but sometimes the organist, Mr. Briers would tell my father someone was playing the organ. I would be questioned, but I didn't know anything about it. Maybe we didn't put the stops back right. Mum was the word! It didn't stop us from going back to the church and doing it again. We felt very exhilarated after doing all of this. A sense of power!

Sister and Friends

Lila lived at our house as often as Judy did. Lila came on our holidays with us too. Lila is Shirley's best friend. Both sets of us were like the "Bobbsy Twins." We were always together. Judy and Lila are just like our sisters, being the same age and all. The only thing Judy and Lila didn't do was sleep at our house! Not that I can remember anyway.

Judy and I would be doing our things and a lot of times Shirley and Lila wanted to join in with us. We told them they were too young. Three years' difference was a big gap in age for Judy and me!! Shirley and Lila were too little for us to be bothering with them. We didn't want to be playing with them at all. We ran away from Lila and Shirley a lot, hiding on them so they couldn't find us. Then we would carry on, on our merry way. Until the next time it happened! We didn't know why they wanted to hang around with us! We did our things together and they could do their things by themselves too! Shirley and Lila said we always had more fun.

Lila's grandparents lived at her house on Pleasant Street. They moved to North Sydney from Newfoundland. Lila's mother was kept busy with a big family to look after. Ken, Effie, John, George, Lila, the twins, Sharon and Elaine, and twins again, Lloyd and Larry. They are all very good looking. Some have blonde hair and the others, black hair. They are a very close family. Each of the kids has a best friend too.

On a Saturday morning we might run up the stairs of the parish hall as fast as we could. Rushing in to play shuffleboard and trying to get the basketballs in the net. The basketballs were so heavy and we could never get them quite in. Our arms would get so sore from trying to centre the ball. It wasn't an easy thing to be doing! We would keep trying and trying. There was definitely an advantage to being a Minister's daughter. I could get into the church and the parish hall whenever I wanted. Daddy would say that it was alright. It kept us out of his hair I am sure! The doors were never locked. The church and parish hall doors always open. There was no one else around when we were there, so we could do whatever we wanted. Just like playing in the church.

On my first day of school, I went with Judy and her brother, Donnie. Donnie was a whole year older. It was an exciting day! Judy knew some of the teachers as she had already attended kindergarten and grade one at Central School. She knew it all! Everything about everything! The school smelled of fresh paint and floor cleaner as Judy and I walked in the door. Sawdust was sprinkled on the floor when the janitor swept up the dirt. We were assigned to our classrooms and to our very own desks.

There was an inkwell in every desk. A drawer to keep your books and papers in. Attendance was taken every day. You had to put up your hand when the teacher took the roll call. In high school we said "here" when our names were called.

Friends with Allie Jeans's brother Arthur, Alice (centre) and her sister Shirley (right)

We were given brown paper book covers that had to be specially folded to keep our books looking nice. We wrote our names and the title of the book on the front cover. There was no mistaking your book for someone else's. We got checkmarks on our answers if they were right, by the teacher. A silver or gold star at the top of the page if your work was really good. The teacher helped you if you needed her. Some boys liked to tip up the desks when the teacher wasn't looking, then down again with a big thud. You had to have a note from your mother to be excused from class. We made our own notes to each other that we would pass. Sometimes we got caught doing it. It didn't take very long to get to know everyone in the different rows. When we had been going a bit, a bunch of us found gas masks in the school basement. The soldiers left them there after the war. The soldiers were stationed at the school during the Second World War. We would try on the masks. They were all different sizes. You felt really closed in when you had one on, like you couldn't breathe.

School Days

I met so many kids at school. Many I had already met at church and the rest from the other streets. There were separate doors for the girls and boys and separate washrooms. I couldn't figure out the door bit. Marbles were the big thing at recess. Owning a steelie or winning one was a really big deal. We would bounce them off the cement of the school basement.

We would sing our favourite rhymes as we skipped. We would sing "Teddy Bear Teddy Bear Turn Around," "Skip to My Lou," and "One Potato Two Potato" ongoing. We skipped with single and double ropes. Jumping in was a big feat. It was natural to get your legs tripped up. The boys would be getting into scraps with each other. Pushing and shoving.

Racing after the girls. The girls pulling each other's hair was a given. We would be making and throwing snowballs in the winter. We didn't have enough time at recess to make a snowman. Sometimes the boys would put a rock in the middle of a snowball. Throw it they did. The girls would be crying if they got hit. Getting the strap was greatly feared. Some teachers were better at it than others. They knew where to hit. I was told that it stung and their hands would be red for a long time after. We saw their hands. Three of my friends had it happen and everyone knew for the rest of their lives! Going to the principal's office wasn't a good thing either. Everyone knew!

One of my classmates had her hand up to go to the bathroom. The teacher didn't notice fast enough and she wet her pants in her seat. Oh my! She was so embarrassed and started to cry. The teacher took her out of the classroom into the hall. When they came back in it was quickly forgotten. We went on with our work.

During class, we would practice and practice our letters. Lowercase and capitals. Then we got to writing them. In our best writing, of course. Over the blackboard the letters were all displayed. We try to copy them just the same. Then we got to practicing our names. The first name alone, perfecting it. Then the last and then together. We wrote with a right slant, left slant or straight up and down. I preferred the right slant. I really liked it when we learned to write a letter. The date, the salutation, the body of the letter, the closing and your name. Your address in the left hand corner of the envelope. Maybe that is why I still like writing letters today. Judy doesn't like writing them. She likes to phone. I don't mind.

At recess time, we would be rushing to Vatcher's store to fetch our penny candy. Mr. Vatcher was Gwen, Moira, Shirley, Susie and Nancy's father. Five or six pieces of candy or gum for a penny. We are always in a line waiting for our turn to be served. And in excitement! On the way to school, you could also stop off at Vickers, Farrell's, or Johnny Ings' stores. Depending on the way you were coming from. Black licorice cigars and pipes, cracker jacks, double bubble gum. Caramilk and Cherry Blossom bars. Licorice nibs and rosebuds. Wax lips and sugar cones too. I loved them all. We might trade them after we left the store. Jabalee's, Rahey's, and Lemoine's were the biggest grocery stores. Our parents would buy food from all of them. Going in person or having it delivered to your house. Our fish we got at Kelly's. You would find Mr. Healey serving at the counter. The Catholics had fish on Wednesdays and Fridays for their suppers. Daddy being a minister, we do the same thing at our house. It wasn't one of my favourite meals.

The Kite and the Kindness

One day, walking home from school, I ran into Ronnie Hiscock. He lived a couple of doors down on Pierce Street. He had the distinction of being an uncle, at age nine, to his sisters' children. Ronnie was very proud of that. He would tell everybody about it. He was out flying his kite in the back field behind our house. It might have been the first time I ever saw a kite. He made it all by himself. Ronnie said he would make one for me. He went off and came back with sticks and newspaper to cover the frame and make the tail. A big ball of string, too. It didn't take him any time at all. Then we ran and ran as fast as we could to get the kite up in the air. Up and down it went. Sometimes hitting the ground. It wasn't an easy thing to be doing. Standing still when there was a good wind. Watching it soar! What a thrill it was to have it flying and flying, up and up in the air! Then, it would nose dive and the running to get it back. By the time we headed for home, the kite looked all battered up and we were winded. What fun it was! Exciting!

Ronnie was the boy who told me my dog, Prince, was killed by a car. I was on my way back to school after lunch one Tuesday. He saw it happen at our corner. He was so kind when he told me. I was so upset. I rushed home and found out Daddy had put Prince in the doll house on the bunk bed. He was lying there with a blanket on top of him, so still. Daddy told me Prince was in heaven. It is amazing how close you can become to your pets. Maybe even closer than most people. They are always there for you. They accept you the way you are no matter how you are feeling.

Ronnie went into the service after high school. He was stationed in Ontario. He died in a car accident coming back to North Sydney one summer for a visit. Ronnie left a wife and four children. I will always remember the wonderful afternoon with the kite and his kindnesses. The kite day was so special!

Shirley Temple

It was always so quiet when Judy and I were alone in the parish hall. Not like a regular day or a Sunday. Things always going on. Downstairs and upstairs and up on the stage. Singing, to beat the band. We danced and twirled! Judy, Joan Peters and I wanted to take tap dancing lessons. It was probably because of all the tap dancing we saw at the show. Mum arranged for Shirley Banfield to give us our lessons. Shirley was my patrol leader in Girl Guides. We got our black patent leather shoes with clickers on the toes. How we loved to tap them! We danced to "The Sheik of Araby." Our only piece! We had three lessons and soon got tired of it. The steps kept getting harder. I never forgot the steps or the piece. Shirley Temple we were not!!

The Cinema

On a Saturday afternoon, Judy and I would be lined up in front of the Odeon Theatre with everybody else. It was a fun time seeing who was in line, gabbing and deciding who was going to sit with who? Phil Medjuck was sure to be there on a Saturday smiling and laughing with everybody else. He was so much fun and so nice.

Being met by Mr. Farr, the owner, in the lobby or outside the theatre door. He was a tiny man as was his wife. He was always very pleasant and smiley. He insisted on very good behaviour in the theatre. The little kids would head for the front rows. Couples would run into the theatre and rush for the back seats. That's where the heavy necking took place! Everyone knew everyone else's business in the movie theatre. Who was going with who? Who was sitting with who they weren't supposed to be sitting with! Girls saving a seat. Hoping someone special would sit with them.

Mr. Andrea was in a room behind us, showing the movie with the projector. We watched the cartoon, the trailer and the main feature. We paid ten cents for the Saturday matinee. Twelve cents for the weekdays. When the price was raised to seventeen cents, no one could believe it. The ushers would escort you down the aisles with their flashlights when you were late. They would escort you outside if you were misbehaving. Everyone would be looking then and shushing each other.

There was always a big cheer when the cartoon started. We ate our popcorn and chocolate bars and drank our pop as we watched. We all had our favourite movie stars. If it was a musical, like "Singing in the Rain," we would be dancing and singing on the way home. It took our eyes awhile to get used to the light when we came out.

We would be hurrying home for supper on the weekdays. Rushing up to our church on Saturdays to see the bride coming out. Standing and waiting! Judy and I did a lot of that!

On Tuesdays, Judy would come over to my house after school. She came every other day of the week too! Tuesday was a special day! My mother made bread and rolls. I can still taste them. The butter melting all over them. When my Granny G. was visiting, she and my mother would make them together. Granny G. used no recipes. Strictly from scratch and how the dough felt in her fingers. There was no trial and error.

Mum baked a lot. Banana and lemon breads, sugar cookies, haystacks, lemon pies and gingersnaps, on and on. Twice a year, the students were told to ask their mothers to make fudge for the Central Home and School sale. My mother would get so frustrated. As hard as she tried, even with different recipes, she couldn't get it to set. Mum was always using her candy thermometer. Past the soft boil, up to the hard boil over and over again. Let's say nothing worked! Judy's mother was an excellent fudge maker. The fudge would sell for a nickel a bag. It was quite a treat if you happened to get a piece of chocolate fudge, especially with walnuts. My mother didn't like fudge days. I couldn't blame her. Watching her do it time after time!

Fresh Bread and Crisp Clothes

Monday was washing day for most everyone. The clotheslines would be filled to overflowing blowing in the breeze. A competition of sorts to see who got their clothes out on the line first and who had the whitest wash! On winter days, the sheets and clothes would be as stiff as boards. You could cut yourself on them if you weren't careful. Always making sure to bring in all of the clothes pegs. Boy, did they smell nice! After bringing them in and thawed a bit, they limped. My mother had a wringer washer. Coming home at lunchtime, the kitchen floor would be covered with water. I remember my sister, Shirley, getting her fingers caught in the wringer. What excitement that was!

The Bats in the Belfry

Judy and I spent hours and hours running around our house playing cowboys. Heading our sides yelling, "giddy up." Pretending we were Roy Rogers and Gene Autry. Roy Rogers and Dale Evans were our favourite cowboy and cowgirl. We would be outside long after dark. Some nights, we would walk down to the front of the church and look up at the steeple. We were looking for bats. We always had our hands over our heads just in case we saw any. We were afraid of our hair getting gucky. Judy and I heard by word of mouth, you would have to get your hair all cut off, if they struck. We were terrified of them, but it was daring. We never did see any but we could hear them. The funny noises they made.

Playing Dress Up

I like to play in my parents' bedroom. Just me, by myself, when no one else was around. I'd rush to the closet to have a look. I loved to try on my mother's shoes. Let's just say they were too big on me but I tried them on just the same. I liked the noise the heels make on the floor. My ankles leaning to the sides. A little bit hard to stand upright for any length of time. Into mummy's drawer I would go for nylons with seams and a garter belt to hold them up with. Putting them on was not an easy thing. Getting the lines straight in the backs of them. A little bit baggy and saggy, maybe more than a little. I liked to try on my mother's full-length slips and bed jackets. So soft and frilly. I'd find myself sitting in front of the mirror. Slowly, taking the things out of mummy's jewelery box. Beads and choker necklaces all tangled up to wrap around my neck. A little bit tricky getting the clasps to close. So many different earrings to choose from. Screwing them on my ears and being careful not to be pinched or have them hanging off. Rings on my fingers. Lipstick and a powder puffed face. A hat with a veil and feather on my head. I looked very colourful and fancy. All grown up!

Driving with Miss Cape Breton

Judy's mother would take us for drives in the Ford family car. She was always willing to take us for a ride. Or, she was going and wanted to take us with her. At that time, she was one of the few lady drivers in North Sydney. Mrs. Clark was also named Miss Cape Breton when she was sixteen years old. Mrs. Clark is such a beautiful lady. She always has her lipstick on. We would drive the circle from North Sydney to Sydney Mines. A favourite ride. We would drive down King Street, left on Commercial and on past St. Elizabeth's Hospital. The harbour on the right of us. Up Greener's Hill and into the Mines. Passing the Sydney Mines post office and through Centreville again and on home. We would also go out the old road. A drive to Sydney! A place much bigger being a city and all. We would always go up and down Charlotte Street. So many more stores and people about. People doing their shopping and their business. Ladies carrying their brown shopping bags. The lovely clothes displayed so nicely in the store windows. Sometimes, we might stop in and have refreshments at the Isle Royal Coffee Shop or the Diana Sweets.

Bernadine

The Clarks. Allie Jean (left), Judy's Dad, Judy, Donnie, and mom

If we weren't driving in the car, we were in Judy's front room. The record player was in there. The song "Bernadine" was played so often, Judy's little sister, Norma thought that that was what the record player was called. "Bernadine." Norma was about two and a half at the time. Norma was always talking and pointing to Bernadine. Donnie, Judy and I would dance. Donnie taught us to slow dance and jive. We loved the jiving. Donnie was a great dancer. We sang along to the tunes. The room would be jumping. We'd be racing up and down the stairs. Maybe getting something in Judy's bedroom or going to the bathroom. We would be answering the telephone and making telephone calls ourselves. The telephone would be passed back and forth and the same gossip would be repeated. Maybe talking about going to someone's house or meeting at one of the hamburger shops. Sometimes Judy, Donnie, her parents and I would play canasta at the kitchen table. The Clarks taught us to play. The game would go on and on. Then we would play it again!

Dad's Ministerial Duties

My father spent a lot of time on his church work. The church services, four every Sunday, the Men's Club, the Vestry meetings and choir practices. Daddy picked out all the hymns for the services. His favourite hymns were "How Great Thou Art" and "I Hunger and I Thirst." Daddy also visited the hospitals. He gave communion to people who were shut in, those not well enough to come to church. Daddy visited every family who belonged to St John's Church. He would encourage the parents and children to attend church and the different groups. He wanted everyone to be members of the Church of England. That was the only church for Daddy. He was always home for meals and he liked them on time. Noon time and 5 o'clock on the dot. When Daddy came home from visiting the T.B. Sanatorium, he would take off his suit jacket and sweater and hang them on the clothesline to air. To get rid of the germs. As suppertime, he would tell us a bit about the illnesses, the people he saw that day. It wasn't great when you were trying to eat your supper.

Dad at Home

My father loved flowers. In particular, dahlias and gladiolas. One spring, he went out on the old dirt road and dug up three baby maple trees. One for me, Shirley and my little brother, Tommy Arthur. He planted them on the side of the house facing Pierce Street. We watched them grow and we watered them when we remembered. Daddy liked putting up the hood on the car and checking the oil. He liked to top it up. He also liked to kick the tires with his foot. He could tell if they were all right. My daddy always wore black suits and a black bib attached to his white collar. Black shoes and black socks. I must not forget his black hat with a brim that he would tip to everyone. This was Daddy's year round wardrobe. In the summer, on our holidays, he would wear a straw hat. The only time he didn't wear his black one. He would take off his shirt or roll up the sleeves of his shirt, to get a little tan on holidays. He would read and say his prayers sitting on his wooden lawn chair.

The Minister's Wife

Allie Jean's mother, Blanche Hodder, née Garland

I never ever saw my mother in pants, shorts, a swimming suit or wearing a bathing cap. A minister's wife wasn't expected to be doing this. No red lipstick, either! Mummy did wear a little bit of orange lipstick that turned pink. It wasn't too noticeable. I was really surprised, when we had a visit from another minister and his family. Finding out that a minister's wife smoked and went bowling! I just couldn't believe it! It was a very unusual thing for her to be doing I thought!

Special Visitors

Confirmation day, Roberta and Allie Jean (right)

We always had people visiting. There were many trips to the airport, the train station and the wharf. Some visitors came in their own cars. It was always fun when the ministers, their wives and kids came. We would visit back and forth having a meal at each other's place and playing. Our parents talked and talked. The ministers were from the other towns in the Cape Breton Deanery. It was always a big thing when the Bishop came. We had to be especially good when the Bishop came and on our very best behaviour. Quite something for me to be doing. Shirley and I would help get the table ready for his visit. All of the best china and silverware would be put out. He would come for Confirmation service.

When you were twelve we were confirmed and then you were able to take communion with your parents. We took special classes before the confirmation. We all felt very grown up then. The girls wore white dresses and a veil over their heads. The boys wore their suits. Sometimes adults were confirmed at the same time. The churchwould be filled to overflowing when the Bishop came. He was as near to God as anyone could be, my Daddy said. The Bishop would carry his staff and wear his purple robes and white surplus. He wore a miter on his head. The Bishop was always very friendly. The Bishop lived in Halifax and his church was All Saint's Cathedral.

The Cousins

It was always a big occasion when the relatives came to visit. Ruth and Jean coming from Toronto, Ontario, by car, with Aunt Elsie and Uncle Wallace. Aunt Laura, Uncle Tom, Joan, the oldest, Tommy and Alice Carmelita Blanche coming by steamer from Gaultois. They would stop off on their way to Montreal for a holiday and stop off again on their way back. Uncle Tom left his car in our garage over the winter. It was always great seeing them all. We would always go to the beach when they came. Aunt Laura would drive us to Sydney and we would have our lunch at the coffee shop in the Isle Royal Hotel. We also looked in the shops.

One summer, when we were in Parrsboro, they stopped off to see us at our cottage we were staying at. They didn't stay too long a time but we did go to the beach and had a little visit. Tommy and Tommy Arthur were almost the same age. Three months separating them.

Tommy Arthur was the older one. Uncle Tom and Aunt Laura always brought nice gifts for us. One Easter time, after they moved to Montreal, they sent a beautiful fruit basket. It was the first time we got to see and taste pistachio nuts, cashews and figs. I loved them all. Fancy, clear wrap covered the basket and a fancy bow on the top of it. Candies in the basket, too.

Grandfather and Grandmother Hodder

Relaxing at the beach with grandmother Amelia Jane Hodder, née Snelgrove

About a year and a half after we moved to North Sydney, my Granny and Grandfather Hodder came to live here too. They lived in one side of a red duplex house on Beacon Street. Their house was about two blocks from our house. Granny and Grandfather were nice and handy to us. Miss MacDonald, my teacher, lived across the street from them. They were alongside of Vooght's big, black, beautiful, house with the big veranda. Granny and Grandfather came from Toronto Ontario. They had been living upstairs in my Aunt Elsie and Uncle Wallace's house.

Grandfather was from Grate's Cove, Newfoundland and was used to being near the sea. He liked the salt sea air and to hear the fog horn blowing. He was a fisherman for a lot of his life. Grandfather said it was a really hard way to make a living. He was a very good carpenter.

Grandfather made a doll house for Judy and me. It had a bunk bed in it. He didn't make it fast enough for me. I was always asking when it was going to be finished. Grandfather took his time. Like snail pace for me. But it was nice when he finished it. Judy and I were so pleased. We put a curtain in the window. The doll house was next to our garage.

Grandfather had also worked at the shipyards in Halifax at one time. Grandfather, a small, plump, man who always had a smile and a twinkle in his eye. Quite quiet though. My Mummy liked to tease him and he would say "now, Blanchie," and laugh. Grandfather liked to whittle and make fish nets when he was sitting outside. His friend, Mr. Caines, who lived on the top of King Street would come down and they would whittle and make nets together, passing the time.

My Granny made up for Grandfather's shyness. Granny was like a house on fire. She was interested in everything and very religious. Education was very important to her, for her children and grandchildren. Granny loved to buy dresses, purses and shoes to keep up to date. Granny G. did as well. It got to be a competition of sorts with Granny. Granny had so many hats she tried on, me doing it too! She always liked to look very nice when she went out. Granny made sure Grandfather looked nice, too.

When Granny was younger, my second cousins Myrtle and Walt told me she was a very beautiful woman. They said she had a lot of suitors. She loved to be complimented on her outfits. How she blushed in embarrassment when people make a nice comment. Granny loved the compliments. Granny has violet eyes and very smooth skin. She always used Camay soap and Pond's face cream. She had long white hair down to her waist. Granny put it in a knot on the top of her head. She used bobby pins to keep it in place without having to look in her mirror to do it. Granny kept her money in a change purse inside the left pocket of her brassiere. It was her safe place to keep it! We were really lucky if she gave us some change! If we were good! Granny G. usually gave us a fifty cent piece for not doing anything.

Granny and Grandfather came to our house quite often. We all went to church together. I sat in the choir. Daddy did the prayers, the preaching and the singing. Sometimes, after church, Granny and Grandfather came for Sunday lunch, our big meal of the day. We usually had chicken, beef or a pork roast with vegetables and rolls. Also served with applesauce or cranberry sauce. The fruit bowl was always in the center of the table. Bananas, my favourite!

Granny Garland

Baby Alice with "Granny G.", Alice Garland, née Lee

Granny liked to decorate, and redecorate, moving the furniture all around the place. She liked to choose wallpapers and have tea parties and go to them as well. Granny and Grandfather loved to watch the programs on television. Especially Lucille Ball in "I Love Lucy". Granny loved to read the Cape Breton Post and the Halifax Chronicle Herald. She liked to keep up on the actors and actresses. Judy and I would stop off and see Granny and Grandfather some days after school, for tea and cookies. They didn't mind us dropping by.

It was always a fun time when Granny G. came to visit. She spent equal time at our house and with my cousins in Gaultois. Then later on when Aunt Laura and Uncle Tom moved to Montreal. Granny G. always came with gifts in her suitcase, for each one of us. Granny G. was 4'10" tall and wore size four shoes. Granny G. always said she would like to be taller in the next life, as she couldn't reach the kitchen cupboards! She was a little bit plump and when she laughed hard her tummy would jiggle up and down. She would be pressing her hands down on her stomach trying to make it stop. We would all be laughing because it happened a lot!

Granny G. liked dressing up like Granny Hodder. Both grannies always looked very nice in their dresses. Granny G. knitted lots of mittens and white socks without a pattern. She liked playing 45's and Old Maid with us kids. There was always lots of laughing going on when we played. Granny G. went to church and to the tea parties with my mother. Different church ladies would have them in their homes. My mother would have tea parties too. Granny G. would help get the tea party ready with Mum. The ladies were always very nicely dressed. Wearing their hats when they came to our house.

Granny G. was a very good cook. She liked to make sure that everyone had plenty to eat. After a big meal, she would be serving leftover chicken or beef sandwiches almost as soon as you got up from the table. Everyone was so full! No one could eat another mouthful! Granny

G. was a very good hostess and loved to see the company come, as we all did. As soon as someone arrived, the tea kettle was quickly put on the stove. We were sad when it was time for her to leave. We had so much fun with her. Granny G. loved to fly. You couldn't get Granny Hodder on an airplane. She was too afraid.

Bringing in the Sheaves

When we lived in Port Morien, the Sunday School kids would carry sheaves up to the church from the parish hall. It felt like such a big hill to climb to the church. I was only five or six at the time. We sang,

"Bringing in the Sheaves" all the way up to the top. Singing the verse over and over. The churchmen took the sheaves from us when we reached the door and placed them around the church. Cabbages, apples, turnips, potatoes, carrots, parsnips, hay and corn stalks we saw all through the church. Bread placed nicely on the altar, and vegetables on the lectern and the pulpit. The families who had farms brought them for the Thanksgiving service. It was the service to thank God for the harvest. The vegetables and the apples were given to the needy families after church.

The Cenotaph

On Remembrance Day, we had the day off school. Poppies were given out by our teachers in the classrooms. We memorized "In Flanders Fields" in our class and wrote it out in good writing. The Girl Guides, the Boy Scouts, the Brownies, the Sea Cadets, the Air Cadets marched in the Parade with the Veterans. They marched down Commercial Street to Archibald Avenue to the Cenotaph. The Mayor and the council men and the ministers were there waiting for them to arrive. Judy, Joan, Roberta, Jean MacDonald and I would be there. A special service was said and poppy wreaths were placed at the Cenotaph. I remember how cold it was standing there. I noticed the many medals on the Veterans' jackets. They all looked so sad. It wasn't a good thing what they were remembering, I am sure. It was a very quiet occasion. All of us remembering the men who lost their lives for us. Some of the men belonged to St. John's and their names were engraved on two plaques in the church. Men from the First and Second World Wars who gave up their lives for our country, so that their fellow man could have better lives. We saw some of their relatives in church.

Christmas Morning

On Christmas morning, our stockings would be filled with oranges, apples, walnuts, hazelnuts and almonds in the shell. I would hang up my Lyle stocking. I remember getting a little clear glass train one year with lots of tiny candies. Santa would fill the stockings and he would leave the toys. I remember getting a spin top and a dolly. I wanted the doll so badly. The rest of the gifts came from your parents, grandparents and aunts and uncles. At Christmas, the dining room table was always set with the best china dishes, silverware and a white tablecloth. Like it would be for Sundays and company. A red or green paper napkin would be at each place. Shirley and I would help Mum set the table. When I was nine I wanted a baby buggy so badly. That is all I talked about. We kids would be in bed at half past six waiting for Santa to come. Lying there, it seemed forever. Imagining you could hear him coming. Then thinking he did! I would go out to the top of the stairs and ask if Santa came yet. The answer was always, "no." "Go to sleep." Santa only comes if you are asleep. I heard someone at the door before too long. I got up and saw Mr. Bond bringing in my baby buggy, from his store. Was I upset! I didn't want the buggy then. I was very disappointed and let down. I never believed in Santa again!

Choir

We had a very big Junior Choir at St John's church. When you were nine, you could join. It was a big occasion when we got to wear our red cassocks and our white surpluses. We wore our street clothes until the ladies of the church made the gowns up for us. We looked like angels but that wasn't always the case. It was hard to sit still during a church service and not talk to each other. There would be pushing, shoving and whispering in the choir room. We would line up two by two downstairs, bounding up the stairs like a herd of elephants and into the church. Daddy would be shushing us as we went by him on the landing. The congregation was waiting for us to come in.

I was always at the front of the line with Roberta because we were shorter than everybody else. The taller kids were always at the back. When you turned seventeen you could join the Senior Choir and then get to wear black cassocks. We had really good singers on the Senior Choir. Jack and Irene Moore, Mr. and Mrs. Shadforth, Mrs. Manger, Mr. and Mrs. Harris, Leslie Hitch and Mrs. Angel. They sang solos and duets. The choir generally sang an anthem. They sang in the choir for a long time. Never missing a Sunday of church.

We sometimes dropped our collection and we would be pretty well down on all fours looking for it under the kneeler. Sometimes the kneelers would fall over. Everybody would be looking then! We weren't allowed to chew gum but the occasional mint would be passed. As we sat in the choir pews facing each other, we might sneak a peek out at the congregation and up to the balcony. Looking to see if there was someone special up there that day. Ronnie would always be sitting up there smiling down at us. We were pretty good singers and during communion we had to be reverent, said my daddy. Being very quiet! We would sing three or four communion hymns as the adults came up the chancel steps and then returned to their seats. We sang "I Hunger and I Thirst" at every Communion service.

Special Occasions

On Palm Sunday, palm crosses were given out that the Altar Guild ladies had made. At Easter time, we would be dressed in our best clothes. A new dress, or new suit and short white gloves on our hands. Maybe, a new pair of shoes. At Christmas time and Easter, we got to sing all of our favourite carols and hymns. "Silent Night," "Carol Sweetly Carol," "We Three Kings," "Gloria in Excelsis," "He is Risen," and "Ride on Ride On in Majesty." We knew them all and mostly by heart. Daddy liked everyone singing as loud as they could and he liked a big choir turnout. We practiced over and over until we got the hymns right. We would sing at the top of our lungs.

Some of the choirboys were servers helping Dad and Rev. Turner. Reverend Turner was Daddy's curate, his helper. Rev. Turner was like a second father to my sister, little brother and me. St John's had a large congregation and piles of kids in Sunday School. Two ministers were needed to do the church work with so many people. Rev. Davies was the curate at St. John's before Rev. Turner. Mrs. Davies was very nice and we played with their kids John, Margaret and Linda. We had so much fun socializing in the choir and in our other groups. We were all excited to see each other when we were getting in and out of our gowns. Betty, Thelma and Joan Kinslow ("I am going to be an actress"), Lois MacDonald, Betty Hillier and her cousin Gloria Rose, Jan Stephens, the Vatcher sisters and their very pretty mom, Isabel Blagdon, Evelyn Rooke, Jean Voutier, Clarence and Norma May, Nina and Ruby Evans, Bob Standing, Joan and Jean Peters, Bob Patey, Bill Ingraham, sister Shirley, Adelin Young, Thelma Hatcher, Joyce and Eric Sibley to name some of them. We also sang at the lovely weddings. We got to see the bride's and bridesmaids' dresses. It wasn't unusual to sing at the early service and come back for the eleven o'clock one or Evensong service at 7 p.m. and do it all over again. We attended Sunday School at two o'clock each Sunday.

Songs We Sang

There were songs we always sang. "You Are My Sunshine," "Good Night Irene," "Row Row Row Your Boat," "Eenie Meenie Miney Mo," "An Itsy Bitsy Spider," "Polka Dot Bikini," "Farmer in the Dell," "Pussy Cat Pussy Cat," "I'm Gonna Sit Right Down and Write Myself a Letter," "Campfire's Burning," "Twinkle Twinkle Little Star," "Oh My Darling Clementine," "Ebb Tide," "Rags to Riches," "A Hundred Barrels of Beer on the Wall," "Buttermilk Sky," "Polly Put the Kettle On," "This Land is Your Land," "The Impossible Dream."

The First TV Sets

I can remember when seeing 'snow' and the test pattern was quite something. I am talking about television. We saw the television sets for sale at Thompson and Sutherlands. People sitting in front of a television screen with just fuzzy snow and the volume turned up so loud. Hoping to see a picture of something or maybe hearing something! There was usually only a shadow and you couldn't make out what it was. We were waiting for the CBC TV and CJCB TV stations to come on the air.

We traveled to Maine one summer and we would count the number of television antennas we saw. At night, Shirley and I would be straining our eyes looking through the car window. Looking for a television screen with a picture through someone's window. It was a pretty difficult thing to do with the car moving so quickly.

Everybody was excited about television coming to Cape Breton Island! We had one of the first television sets on our street. I can remember lots of faces peeking through our living room windows to catch a glimpse of the first show, that night. My father was up and down adjusting the rabbit ears. Getting a clearer picture. No one else was allowed to touch them. It took some messing around to get the picture right.

When the two stations aired, we would be up and down turning the channel button. "Burns and Allen" was the first show that we saw. The programs came from New York to our local stations. We all got caught up with the many programs. "Gunsmoke," "Father Knows Best," "I Love Lucy," "The Mickey Mouse Club," "Leave it to Beaver," "The Andy Griffith Show" and Bonanza. My mother loved "Liberace" and his song, "I'll be seeing you." Mum never missed Liberace's program. We kids watched it too. His brother, George, never said a word all the way through the program. Just playing his violin and smiling! Dad, Mum and Tommy Arthur loved to watch the wrestling. Tommy Arthur would be punching the chesterfield cushions. Television didn't stop us from going to the movies at all. That's where we met our friends. Our mothers would be home still listening to "Laura Limited," "The Happy Gang," "Ma Perkins," and "Amos and Andy" on the radio. It didn't cost much money for us to have our fun.

The Northside Forum

The Northside Forum. Hurrying there on a weekday and on a Saturday morning. Bundled up keeping out the cold. It seemed to be colder inside the building when we got in. Joyce and Reg Allen were always there to greet us. Then the business began getting on our skates and lacing them up. I had to have ankle supports in mine. I seemed to take longer than everyone else. I wore tube skates, but Judy had figure skates. I had tried them, but only managed to fall down. I didn't like the picks. All of the well-known figure skating champions owned them. Judy and I got to see Barbara Ann Scott and Michael Kirby at the Sydney Forum. Barbara Ann was so beautiful with her blond hair and red lipstick. In high school, we traded them in for Bauer racer skates. Did we feel like big deals floating along on the ice! Would they go!

The music was playing non-stop. Lots of kids skated along. Some of us in pairs holding each other's clenched fists, pressing into each other's sides. Skating this way kept you from falling down on the ice and you had a nice rhythm. You would be skating along and someone might tap you on the shoulder interrupting the skate. Off you would go with them. You would feel popular and important if this happened, skating off with them. "Hernando's Hideaway," "Green Door" and "Memories are Made of This" still ring through my ears. There was always great music, great pieces to skate to. Around and around we went. A few parents would come to the weekday skate. Let's just say Judy's mother and Mr. Ashley from our church, rarely missed. All eyes would be on them as they twirled around. They made it look so easy. Mr. Ashley must have been seventy at the time. We kids would try and keep up with them but we couldn't. A hot chocolate was a welcome treat from the snack bar. We would skate for two hours straight. Halfway through, the rink rats would come out and clear off the snow with their big shovels. Then they would water it. Was it slippery when we got back on! Lots of us falling down! The rink rats were great skaters and hockey players. We got to meet the St. Joe's kids at the forum. One of them, Jigger Andrea, became an NHL player!

Driving Lessons

Allie Jean on a break from cruising

Judy's house and her grandfather's house were side by side. We saw a lot of her grandfather. He must have been 80 years old at the time. Judy calls him Grand Dad. Grand Dad would take us out for bumpy rides in his old black Ford with running boards. He drove very slowly so it took a long time to get anywhere. Judy's mother taught the both of us to drive when the time came, out the old dirt road, out to the cemetery. I remember the beautiful coloured leaves as we drove. We had to avoid the many potholes. The dust was always a flying. Judy was always the better driver! Her mother and Judy agreed! Not me! Later, I learned to shift gears, which was the in thing to know how to do. Quite something for a girl to be doing.

Judy's Dad

Judy had a very nice daddy. Judy and her daddy looked so much alike. Mr. Clark was usually very easy to get along with. He also had a great sense of humour. Mr. Clark was always smiling. We would go to Vicker's store when he asked us to, to pick up his "Players," please cigarettes. That is what he called them. They were thirty-one cents a package. He liked to torment Judy by saying, "no ins," and "no outs." When Judy was not allowed to go out and play, Allie Jean was over there trying to get him to change his mind. He said, "no outs," but I told him we wouldn't be gone very long. He liked to get a rise out of us and put off his decision about what we were doing and not doing. We were on "pins and needles"that he wouldn't let her out. After about ten minutes of "no ins, no outs," back and forth, he would change his mind about Judy going out. Were we relieved! He would say it was alright if Judy was with me, the minister's daughter! Judy can do no wrong with me! This happened every time Judy wanted to go out with her girl or boyfriends. He did it, I know, to get us going. Did he laugh when we were leaving! Mr. Clark called Judy's bedroom "Sleepy Hollow." Especially when she would sleep in on a Saturday morning, after a dance the night before. She knew then, it was time to get up! He would keep nattering at her and teasing her until she moved. He loved kidding around with us!

The Town Exhibition

In September, the boys hightail it for the fairgrounds. The exhibition is coming to town. The carnival people are setting up tents, booths and the many rides. The boys maybe getting a chance to help them and get a free ride or two. Judy and I always pay our price of admission! Some of the daring kids sneak in under the fence when no one is looking and they don't have to pay. They never get caught. If you were caught you weren't allowed on the grounds again. Judy and I did it one year and felt so guilty about it, but no one knew. Just us. The many coloured lights flashing on and off, making the fairgrounds look so pretty.

Judy and I like to ride on the tilt a whirl and the merry go round. Some kids get short rides for their money instead of long rides. Not really a very fair thing for the circus man to be doing! The men running the rides are not the cleanest people around and some are pretty scary looking. We stick close to each other all the time holding hands.

One year, Judy's father took us up on the ferris wheel. It was my first time. A very scary ride. He rocked the seat and rocked it when we were at the very top. He was joking around with us but I was terrified. Judy not saying anything too much. The people below us on the ground, looking so tiny. Were we up high! The jolting coming down as each car was being emptied. Holding on for dear life! Me, thinking the bar going across us would open up and we would fall to the ground. The movement churning up my stomach. I didn't get on the ferris wheel ever again after that. One of my schoolmates fell out of the ferris wheel and hurt her back. She wasn't too badly hurt, thank goodness.

A circus man tells us he can guess our weight. A prize to win, if he can't do it. He has a huge scale, not like the scale at our house. We step on it, thinking we have a good chance to win. The man knew right off what we weighed. So quick about it. Disappointing to us! How could he know what we weighed type of thing, right away? Not knowing us or seeing us before. Cotton candy and candy apples sticking to our cheeks and hands. Kids wandering from one ride to another, trying to find something to spend their nickels and dimes on. Five cents for this, five cents for that. We can never quite get the hoops over the wooden milk bottles, standing all in a circle. Our arms just aren't long enough to reach them. Lots of parents and kids playing Bingo. Mrs. Gove and Mrs. Healey always win at the Bingo. Kids and adults in the crowd carrying stuffed animals they have won. The white poodles are a favourite prize.

Judy and I check out the horses and cows in the barns. The barns are not too clean, nice smelling places, but we pat them just the same. Climbing up on the gate to get a closer look at them. The cows, looking so lonely standing there in their stalls. Their eyes looking so sad. Judy and me feeling sorry for them. Ribbons hanging down around their necks on some of them. We see the hearts, diamonds, clubs and spades spinning around on a big wheel. No one seems to be winning very much at that colourful booth.

Our money is gone before we know it! Judy and I like going to the Exhibition. We never know what we are going to be doing next. We are never in any hurry to go home for supper and wanting to come back again right after we have it.

Skipping School

One time, I skipped school with Judy. I should say she did it quite often. I was petrified! The fear of getting caught and having to go to the principal's office. Your parents being called. Having to write sentences on the blackboard. Over and over again. The day, I remember so well. We skipped and high tailed it to the Post Office. As we were going in one door, who was coming out the other? Our Principal, Mr. Kenney. I held my breath. Judy said, "Quick." Up the steps we went. Mr. Kenney didn't see us. Were our cheeks red! Were we worried! Yes we were!! We waited until the coast was clear and then we took off. Back to the school. I never skipped school again!

Christmas Visiting

We go to the Westcott's for our Christmas suppers. They come to our house for New Year's Day. It is always a nice time visiting them.

David's train set is laid out on the basement floor. We sit down on our bums and watch the cars go by. It is a little black train on a big oval track. A red caboose on the back. He puts a little tablet in the engine smokestack and the smoke comes out before you know it. David lets us each put a tablet in. Arthur, Shirley and me. Around and around the cars go. Through a little village. We are soon going cross-eyed. David always shows us his fish flies that he makes. He has lots of them. Very tiny things. All different colours. If you aren't careful you can stab your fingers. David spends a lot of time making them. The Westcott's tree is always very fancy. Mrs. Westcott whips up soap powder and water and puts spoonfuls on the branches. It has to sit awhile to harden. It looks just like real snow. The bubble lights and ornaments look very nice. The white angel with blond hair on top. Mrs. Westcott has a special dessert for Christmas. "Floating Islands." Daddy always asks what the dessert is going to be when we land on the front step. He's hoping! Every year we come, Mr. Westcott takes our pictures on his movie camera. He always shows us the movies from the Xmases before. How we changed each time! My hair is never in place. Not the way I would like it to be. We have a turkey dinner. Chocolates afterwards. David is supposed to be my boyfriend and I am supposed to be his girlfriend. That is what our parents want. It isn't true.

My Special Teacher

Mrs. Buchanan is my teacher in Grade 5. She has a wonderful personality and has the best handwriting of all the teachers. She uses turquoise ink in her pen. She is the only teacher who uses it. Turquoise ink is a new thing. Her writing is very nice to look at and swirly. Mrs. Buchanan makes it look so easy. I had Miss Grant for my teacher in Grade 3 and Grade 4. She always looked very pretty in her outfits. She had lots of them. She always looked very nice. Wearing pretty earrings and red lipstick. I looked at her a lot when she was at the front of the class. One day, she wore sandals on her feet. I never saw shoes like that before. I spotted her toes. My teacher having toes like me. Did I notice them! Big fat ones. She wasn't special to me anymore.

Shoe Toss

I joined Girl Guides when I was ten. Our Girl Guide group is invited to a Sea Cadets dance. It is my first dance. A bit young don't you think? I didn't know how to dance. We all had to wear our uniforms. The dance was at the Yacht Club not too far from the beach. What a big place it is. Lots of kids standing about. There were so many kids you got lost in the shuffle. I didn't see anyone I knew at first but then I spotted Donnie. Finally someone I knew. Someone called out, "girls in a big circle."

Then, "boys in a circle" outside of our circle. We are told to throw our shoes in the middle. Everyone scurrying to take them off. I knew I had a hole in the toe of my right black stocking. I really didn't want to take my shoe off. The hole seemed to get bigger as I stood there. Let's say I was very blushing about it and embarrassed. A knot in my stomach. I didn't let on. I put my left foot on top of my right foot when we stood still. The music begins and we are all moving. We are all bunched up. When the music stops, we have to look for our shoes. There isn't much time to be looking for them. The music starts up again. Over and over and round and round we go. You feel like you want to be sick. So many black shoes. They are all piled up on top of one another. It seemed like years before I find mine. There wasn't one kid who said anything about the hole in my stocking. Maybe no one noticing. I was glad to get my shoes back on and go home!

The Causeway

On a Sunday afternoon, we drive to Port Hastings to see how the Causeway is coming along. Everybody is talking about it! We know that a lot of people don't want it to be happening. Cape Breton won't be an island anymore, they say. We see the men with their big machinerylifting boulders from the mountain and putting them into place in the water. We notice the cars on the other side of the strait lined up having a look too. Soon, we will be driving straight on through. I don't mind that too much because the ferry rides always scare me. Just ropes on either end of the ferry to keep the cars in safe. My father is very careful about how he parks on the ferry. Only five or six cars can fit, unless there is a big truck. Dad likes to get out and have a stroll around when we get going. The rest of us are happy to stay in the car. Cape Breton Island is going to be joinedto the mainland. Cape Breton will always be an island to me, no matter what!

Sunday School Picnic

In June, we got to go to Camp Breton for our Sunday School picnic. One year, we went to Groves Point. Piling into our fathers' cars and meeting there for the fun day. Scrambling out to see who came. What is going on? Racing around the grounds and having a look see. Spruce trees all around. An old dirt road leading down to the lake. We spend some time skipping stones. There are so many flat, round, smooth ones. It is easy to make them go just kerplunk! One skip. Something else again to make them go five and six times. They skim across the water so nicely. So neat!

One time, I stepped on a baby snake wearing my sneakers. What a funny feeling that was. I couldn't stop talking about it. Eerie! I never liked snakes after that. Judy and I pull up big ferns and eat the nuts from the bottoms of them. Judy knows all about it. Really yanking hard to get them out of the ground. We just wipe the dirt off and down they go. There are lots of races going on. Running from this place to that place as fast as you can. The three-legged race is the most fun one. Lots of falling down and tumbling going on. Everyone laughing and screaming. Not running for a prize but to see who can come in first. Daddy throws handfuls of candies to the smaller kids first. Making sure they all get some. High up in the air they go! We are all in excitement trying to catch them when it is our turn. Daddy throws them over and over again. There is a lot of sharing going on.

Our mothers have their picnic suppers laid out on table cloths on the grass. Each family sitting around their own tablecloth. My mother always brings potato salad with hard boiled eggs, apple, and onion mixed in. Tomatoes and cucumber sliced up. Ham, too. A homemade strawberry pie with a crust on the top. Ants to go with it. The Nestle's cream is yummy. Picnic food always seems to taste better when you eat outdoors. Judy always comes along for the picnics. Lila, too. We use the outhouses when we have to go pee. Not a too pleasing place to be going into. The smell is something else. We get in and out of there as fast as we can. So many flies buzzing around and the Simpson's catalogue for toilet paper. We never look down the hole!

Goodbye Billy

Alice MacDonald is my most favourite teacher. Having the same name as me may have something to do with it, too. Miss MacDonald taught Judy's father too. Judy likes to remind me about it all the time. Being close to the teacher type of thing. Sometimes, we get to walk to school with her. There are two Grade 6 teachers. Judy and I have the best one, Miss MacDonald. The other teacher was a real grump. We were doing our arithmetic one morning. Out of the blue, one of the boys started acting up and jumped out the window. Billy was sitting in his seat and the next thing we knew he was gone. We all ran to the window to have a look. No sign of him at all. It all happened so quick like. It took awhile before we settled down to our work again. Such an exciting time! They soon found Billy and he had to go to the principal's office. He didn't like school. He didn't come back.

Family Vacations

My family has very nice summer holidays. My father gets a month's holiday each year. Our holiday is always in July. We have been to Parrsboro, NS three summers in a row. We stay in a cottage there, down by the water. We all get to sleep in one room on bunk beds. We play checkers on a big wooden checker board just outside the cottage door. We row dories and lots of times our oars get caught in the lily pads. What a job getting them untangled. The yellow flowers are so pretty on the lily pads. The beach we go to isn't too far away. Judy came with us one summer. We collected shells, went swimming and walked into town. It was a bit of a walk for us but we made it! A surprise to us! We really enjoyed going to Wheaton's Restaurant. We each bought a bag of dulse for a nickel. We sat at a booth having our pop. My father got us to liking dulse. He said, "dulse is your iodine content." A bit embarrassing if you get some caught in your teeth. I know my mother invited Judy to come to Parrsboro with us so I would have a friend to play with.

Another summer we went to Gaultois, Newfoundland. My mother was born in Gaultois. We boarded the steamer in North Sydney for Porte aux Basques. Then onto another steamer "The Bar Haven" going down the south coast to Gaultois. Another time, Lorna and Judy came with me. I was the only one who didn't get sea sick. Groceries, fresh fruit,

vegetables, milk and the postal mail came with us on the steamer. There were piles of people lined up at the dock as the steamer came in. Kids screaming in excitement. A big event for the people there having the steamer come every ten days. There was the same reaction when we landed at Burgeo and Ramea and the other out ports. Gaultois, is a small place, only about 500 people living there. There are no cars, roads, television sets or telephones like we have in North Sydney. We spend a lot of our time playing 45's and Auction 120 and listening to the radio. We go fishing in a dory catching fish called Connors. I had never heard of them before. There were so many of them swimming around in schools and very easy to land. You put your hook down and right away you have one looking at you on your hook!

We vacationed in Charlottetown, P.E.I. one summer. The Church of England minister there and dad traded houses for the month. It was quite neat. One afternoon, a lady taught me how to swim at the beach. The breast stroke, the side stroke and the back float. I was kicking my feet to beat the band, looking fancy with my foot work for the back float. They were my only swimming lessons. It was very nice of the lady to spend the time with me. Not many Newfoundlanders swim even though we live near the water. No time for them to learn as their time is taken up with the fishing. The rectory in Mahone Bay, Nova Scotia is across the street from the harbour. Shirley and I swam there quite a few times. One day, a lady came to the door and told my mother we shouldn't swim there. The town jumped the sewage into the harbour. You can imagine what we were imagining! Swallowing the water! Yuck! We felt sick to our stomachs! We had to find another place to swim.

In Orangedale, Nova Scotia we stayed at a farmhouse out in the country. No other houses or people around. My mother kept Shirley and me amused with colouring books. Our mother bought every colouring book in the store. It rained the whole month we were there. I never coloured again. It was a lonely kind of place and I didn't want to go back there anymore.

The Drive-In

Going to the drive-in movies was kind of fun. Sitting in your father's car watching the show under the stars. Two dollars for a car load. We left home about 6:45 p.m. After we ate our supper and the dishes weredone.

The drive-in was out in the country, so to speak. We had to drive outthe Sydney highway to get there. After driving about 35 minutes, we saw the cars turning into the driving entrance. The drive-in sign on the right of us. Daddy turned in looking for a spot to park. Round and round we went until he found the right one. We had a bird's eye view of the motion picture screen. He parked near a post that had a box on the top of it. Daddy told us it was the speaker.

We would hear the movie sounds from the little box. Daddy rolled down his window and put the speaker on top of it. Rolling up the window to keep it in place. A lot of noisy static coming out of it. Daddy turned the sound down with the little button on the bottom of it. The speaker stayed that way until the movie started. Then daddy turned it up. There was a playground right in front of the screen. Off, Shirley and I went playing on the swings and slide. Tommy Arthur, being too little, stayed in the car on my mother's lap. Shirley and I kept running back and forth to the car, to make sure our car was still there. Probably, afraid, that our mummy and daddy would get lost.

Shirley and I decided to wait in the car. We soon got tired of the slide. The waiting we did! Waiting and waiting for the show to start. It took such a long time for it to get dark. We were soon tired of sitting in one spot! We climbed back and forth over the car seats. We soon got tired of that, too. We were squirmy! We were wishing for it to get dark. We went to the canteen for popcorn and pop. I spilled my pop on the floor of the car. Was that a mess! The car horns honked and tooted when the picture came up on the screen. Everybody, glad the waiting had stopped. It was just like being at the Odeon Theatre, except we were outside in our car. It started to rain soon into the show and the windows got fogged up. Shirley and I printed our initials on the windows and then wiped them off with our sleeves. It was cozy in the car, but a little bit cramped. It didn't seem like any time at all, mummy and daddy were putting us into our beds. We fell asleep at the Drive In. It must have been nice for them once we konked out!

A different kind of Drive In movie when you are older and go with your friends. You might go with a boyfriend, two couples or a car load of kids. Some boys, sneaking into the Drive In, hidden in someone's car trunk. Once the boys get inside the Drive In grounds, they scramble out. Watching the movie standing up. Let's say, some of us not watching too much of the show. A place to get "hot and bothered" in. It isn't unusual to lose the car you came in, (so many cars everywhere) on the way back from the canteen or the bathroom. So dark and all! It happened to me one time! Yelling your friends' names over and over again to find your way back to the right car. What a line-up of cars, leaving the Drive In. People very impatient and all wanting to leave at the same time. Sometimes, someone would drive off with the speaker. Not a good thing! The driver is responsible for the speaker. Having to pay for a new one.

Fun with the Cousins

My cousin, David, would stop off for a night or two, on his way to or from the University of New Brunswick. David had the distinction of starting university at 15! A science major. He lived in residence and would be taking his personal things to and from home and university. He said he had to have name tags put on all of his clothes. On one visit my father said, "David, you have everything but the kitchen sink in your trunk." David leaned over and pushed aside a few things. Lo and behold, there was a kitchen sink! We couldn't believe it! He was the smartest cousin. He did ham operating in his spare time and talked to people all over the world.

One July, our Toronto cousins came to visit. Judy and I showed Ruth and Jean our favourite haunts. They had the time of their lives. We had so much freedom going here and there. We always had our freedom. One afternoon, our parents were out visiting. Joan Peters and Judy were home with us. Ruth thought it would be a good idea to have a Rinso bath. I had never heard of it. We all ran to the bathroom. Out came the box of Rinso. In went the plug. Ruth turned the water on. She poured and poured. The whole box went in. You never saw so many suds and bubbles in your life. The suds were going over the sides of the tub and onto the floor. We were all in the tub. Shirley, too. None of us had a stitch on. That was something we never did. You never showed anyone any part of your body that should be covered up. We laughed and giggled, jumping up and down. It was fun in the beginning until our skin started getting red and stinging. We didn't know how itchy and raw we would get. Shirley and I never did it again! The Rinso bath comes up now and then in conversation and we laugh remembering.

We climbed up Ferris' Hill in search of blueberries. Just up from Angel's Foundry. Our only place to pick them. It is such a big hill. We never thought we were going to make it to the top. Judy knows where the wild pears are growing. They are very juicy and delicious. We try to pick our berries very carefully, removing the leaves and putting them in our quart bottles. It is a bit hard keeping the white ones out. We see who can pick the most. We sell them for 15 cents a quart. Our mothers usually buy them from us.

Fishermen

The Portuguese boats come to North Sydney every spring and fall. We see the fishermen all over town. The men go door to door looking for catalogues. Their wives use the pictures for patterns for making their clothes. The fishermen aren't very popular when they wash their clothes in the town reservoir and lay them out to dry on the rocks. Our drinking water is never contaminated though. Pottle's Lake has very clean water.

Hosting the Scouts

In 1952, a Boy Scout Jamboree was held in Ottawa for the "Queen's Coronation" year. The Jamboree was for Boy Scouts everywhere. Canada and all of the countries the Queen oversaw at that time. It was a big deal for a Scout to be going. Fortunately, for Judy and me, the Newfoundland troop stayed in the parish hall for several days before heading back to St. John's. They had to wait for the steamer. They slept in their sleeping bags and made their meals in the down stairs part of the parish hall. They made campfires outside and sang their camp songs. I loved the gooey marshmallows on long sticks they shared with us.

The Scouts and their leaders were all very nice. Judy and I became fast friends with two of the Scouts. Bill, the blond one. Ron, with the dark hair. They both had lots of badges on their shirts. I liked Bill but Judy said she was interested in him. Like don't look at him. Hands off! Billwas her property type of thing. I then paid attention to Ron. I can't remember exactly what we did those days! Maybe going down to the wharf and looking at the boats and the kids fishing. Maybe walking up King Street to the train station. Going in and having a look around and seeing who was coming and going. Seeing if there was anyone we knew. We could have been downtown browsing in the windows or having a sundae at the Owl Drug Store. Mimi made the greatest sundaes, floats and milk shakes. Everyone knew us at the drugstore. Mr. Johnson, the druggist, was always friendly when he saw us come in. We did enjoy Ron and Bill's company. Let's just say they were very good looking and two years older. Judy and I were twelve at the time. We were so sorry to see them leave North Sydney. We never thought we would see or hear from them again. We missed them right away. Nine days later, out of the blue, I had a letter from Ron. He said how nice it was to meet me and would I like to write back. Judy didn't like it because she didn't get a letter from Bill. I wrote back the once. I didn't get another letter. We did have a really good time with them.

Our Violins

It was grade six. Professor MacDonald came to the school to enroll students to take violin lessons. His specialty. Up to this point, Judy and I were only interested in banging on the piano. Judy knew Professor MacDonald. He lived on Pleasant Street. Just down the street from us. He has lots of boys. Judy knows them all. Judy thought we should take violin lessons. Fifty cents a lesson. We persuaded our mothers to let us take them. They were a bit hesitant after the tap dancing lessons. After whining and whining about it they said we could. We had our lessons in the parish hall. Did we think we were something! It was quite a thing getting our own violin, bow and case. Rosin for the bow. A music stand for our music to sit on. The violin rest felt really funny under my chin. Professor MacDonald tuned up the violins for us. The piano nearby. There must have been a dozen of us. He would teach us and we would try to take it all in. The sounds we made was nothing to write home about. They didn't seem to improve over time.

In December, we were told we were going to play at the Xmas concert. We were all quite nervous about it and surprised. Not thinking we were ready. We had two pieces to play. It was hard work with the practicing. Shortly after we got on stage and seated, Professor MacDonald came over to Judy, me and a few others. He whispered that he wanted us not to play. To just hold our violins with bows in place and fake it. At first, I didn't know what he was talking about. Then it sank in. How embarrassing! What a let down! Everyone else playing and we were sitting, "pretending." After the concert, we talked and talked about it. We didn't like it, not at all. We got mad and said we were quitting. The next thing we knew Professor MacDonald was calling our mothers and wanting us to start back again. We didn't want to, not ever again. Our mothers weren't encouraging us either. We didn't seem to stick at things too long. Our feelings were very hurt.

At the Beach

We also went to the beach on the outskirts of town. There we had swings with wooden seats and heavy ropes to hold on to. Also a slide and see saws. What a bump you would get if someone jumped off. The beach is a beautiful sandy beach. The water icy cold but we always managed to get dunked. Sometimes in and out a few times before we actually did it. Avoiding jellyfish of course. Getting tangled up in seaweed. We would come out as fast as we could and get our towels wrapped around us. Teeth chattering. We would warm up and then do it all over again. Sand in our ears and hair. Would you believe in our mouths?

When we got our two wheeled bicycles we went to the beach on our own. There is a very scary steep hill going down to the beach. We had some spills, cut knees and scraped elbows. My bicycle was a CCM with "bloom" tires, maroon in colour. It took a lot of pedaling to get it moving. Judy's bike had regular tires so she was always way ahead of me. When we outgrew our bicycles we moved on to hitch hiking to Christie's. We knew most everyone who picked us up. Teenagers with licences or someone's father. It was a very daring thing to get into a car with someone you didn't know. Our parents didn't know about our hitchhiking.

There was fresh water swimming at Christie's. A diving board at the end of the pier. A hamburger stand to boot. All of us girls would gather on a Saturday sunny afternoon sporting our one-piece bathing suits. A Jantzen suit was a must have. Every colour imaginable was seen. All of the girls would lie on their backs, on their towels, for twenty minutes and then flip to the tummy for another twenty, back and forth for the perfect tan. There was suntan lotion that we could buy, but it was quite greasy. Christie's was another place to meet the boys. The boys would be swimming and horsing around and paying some of us some attention or drawing attention to themselves. They might sit near us on our towels. I would call it thrill time! Sometimes, we would get a ride home with a favourite boy on his bicycle crossbar. We were about fifteen minutes outside of North Sydney. We always had a fun time.

French Lessons

When we were in Grade 7, we were all excited about having French for a subject. Mrs. Blane was our teacher as well as teaching us English. After a few classes, everyone was going around saying the French phrases or sentences they learned. *Comme as a vous, tres bien, parley-vous francaise, depechez-vous* come to mind and singing *"Frere a Jacques"*, ongoing. Everyone felt very French saying the words. A little different than how are ya? Dear, darlin, love, what are you doing? How's it going? Or see ya.

Slang

Do any of these expressions sound familiar to you? Dead as a doornail, if looks could kill, bet you a nickel or a dime, nothing further from the truth, heart throb, Newfie nickels, the nitty gritty, keeping my fingers crossed, heads or tails? What a drip, pucker up, having a hairy fit, stringing someone along, they will drop their socks, quick as a wink.

Snails

Judy I liked to go down to the wharf. We climbed down carefully over the big rocks and pulled off the snails. Sometimes we got just a bit wet. Our shoes sometimes getting dunked and squishy! We'd make a little fire with kindling in my backyard. We put some water in our tin cans to cover them. We popped in the snails and cooked them up over the fire. We picked them out one by one, with our bobby pins. Eating them all! Delicious to us!

Halloween

Halloween is coming! Ghosts and goblins! What to wear? I have my mother in a "tizzy", trying to decide for me. Nothing will do! The kids hit the streets right after supper. Is it dark! Scrambling from one house to another for a treat. Remembering from last year the lady who made the delicious candy apples. Heading back there again and hoping for another one. Feeling cold! Smothering in your mask! Eyes squinting! Arm weighted down! All out of breath! Happy to be going home for the sorting. Gobbling up so many candies and suckers, you want to be sick!

Travelling Salesman

A salesman came to our door selling pots and pans. He wants to come in and give my mother a pots and pans demonstration. He tells mom that you didn't need very much water in the pots to cook the vegetables. Cooking that way, keeps in all the vitamins. He sets down a big box on the living room rug. He brings them out one by one. Pots and pans of all sizes, shiny and new. Even a pancake griddle and a juicer. My mother seems quite interested. He asks if he can come back again in a few days and cook our supper. My mother has the groceries waiting when he comes back. The salesman is soon busy in the kitchen. He uses every pot he has with him for our supper meal, even a frying pan. After not too long a time, the food is ready and waiting. It looks like a banquet on the dining room table. Everything is looking very delicious and hot. Tasting the same way too. My mother bought the whole set of pots and pans. Shirley and I like using the juicer. We drink the juice and eat the pulp from the orange halves. My mother can't keep us in oranges.

The Valentine Box

In the lower grades, we always have a valentine box. Miss MacDonald brings in a nice sized box decorated with hearts and doilies. A slit on the top to put the valentines in. The box looks very pretty sitting on her desk. We drop our valentines in, the days leading up to Valentine's Day. Miss MacDonald calls out the names from the little white envelopes one by one. It is such a thrill to get your valentines. Maybe getting one from the boy you like in your class. Maybe not getting one at all, from that special boy, and being disappointed. I wrote, just my initials on my cards in my fancy writing. No one knew who they were from when they opened them up. They couldn't make out my writing. Miss MacDonald made a point about it. I should have printed my name. Embarrassing for me, the whole class knowing!

Shop Hopping

Our Post Office is at the corner of Commercial and Peppett Streets. A great big building with doors on each end. Steps leading up to the building. It is fun to go in and see what is going on. People buying their stamps, and sending packages by parcel post. It is something Judy and I do on a regular basis. We always run into someone we know. We don't race around or anything like that when we are in the Post Office. No one says, "you shouldn't be here" or "go away." You feel very important being in the Post Office. Something like the way you feel about being in the bank. It isn't as much fun in there though. Not really. Having to be quiet was what we did at the bank. People noticing that you are there and wondering why? We visit Maloney's Shoe Store a lot. We like to try the many shoes on. Sitting on the chairs and putting our feet up on the stools. Mr. Groves always gives us a nylon to wear so we don't get the shoes sweaty. I always like the shoes that are too small for me. I had a pair of black patent leather ones with straps around my ankles. I just had to have them. Telling my mother when I got home that they fit me fine. They were oh, so tight! My feet looked good but were they sore!

We buy our good clothes at Bond's store. Joanie Bond's parent's store. Mr. and Mrs. Bond are always happy to see us when we walk in. Always taking notice of us. They help us make our selections. We are in the dressing rooms trying the things on in a turvey. Coming out to look at them in the full-length mirror. Turning this way and that. Do we like the outfit or not? I soon get tired of the trying on. There are so many things to choose from.

Everybody rushes to the Herald Print in September to get their school supplies. The scribblers and books all smelling so new. Judy always talks to Mr. Miller, the owner. We pop in and say hi to Louise Vardy. She's always at the counter at Nova Scotia Light and Power. That's it, just "hi" and we are on our way again. Fowler's Men's Wear is nearby. The guys and our dads buy most of their clothes there. Mr. and Mrs. Fowler go to our church. Mrs. Fowler teaches us sometimes at Thompson as a substitute teacher like Mrs. Gallop does. Mrs. Gallop also tutors students if they need it, at her home. We duck into Steele's and see the Ford cars lined up. Just looking at them from outside and no touching so as not to scratch them. All new and very clean, smelling very nice. Stagg's taxi stand is near the poolroom. Sammy Gorra is usually there waiting to give someone a ride. Judy and I see him quite often as we walk by. He is very cheerful and takes the time to talk to us. Judy and I have never had a taxi ride yet.

The Belmont Hotel

The Belmont Hotel is on Archibald Avenue. A big, busy place. Some people may be staying the night and waiting for the boat to Port aux Basques. Maybe just coming from there and going to someplace else. The Belmont Hotel has many, many rooms. The bathrooms are in the hallways for the most part. People sharing them, so to speak. Mr. Green, the owner, is usually in the lobby greeting everyone. Even us kids. He doesn't mind us dropping by. We just roam around the lobby watching and seeing what is going on. We try out the chairs and couches. Watching people come in with their suitcases. Grant's Hotel is on Commercial Street. Mr. Grant's son Austin, we wave to. We pretty well know everyone. If I don't, Judy is sure to know them.

The Funeral Parlor

Dooley's Funeral Parlor is a very nice looking building. Painted all black, but not too scary looking. A place we generally don't get or want to visit. When we see their hearse go by we run away as fast as we can! When someone dies, we see a black wreath on the front door. The blinds are all closed. Sometimes a person's body may be laid out in the front parlor of their house. Judy and I walk quietly by, when we see a wreath. The ladies bring their cooked things and baked goods to the family. A nice thing to do. If we knew the kids, we didn't say too much about it to them. Not wanting them to feel bad. Just keeping things natural. Sort of easing it all. In Grade 3, one of our classmates died. She had been away sick for a month. Miss Grant told us about her. We couldn't believe it at first. Not being around us anymore, sitting in class. She was very quiet and nice. Ethel Snook was her name.

Saturday Mornings

A lot of Saturday mornings, Judy and I would head for downtown. Our first stop would be to the magazine and tobacco store. Mr. Buchanan, our teacher's husband, would always be behind the counter talking to a few customers. Gentlemen picking up their morning papers and maybe some pipe tobacco. Judy and I would head for the comic book stand. We would be picking them up, reading them and trading them with each other. We are trying to decide which one we want to buy. One we hadn't read, of course. The comics cost 10 cents. We both liked Veronica and Archie. Little Lulu was lots of fun to read. We loved her black ringlets. We would pay Mr. Buchanan our dime and head for the Owl Drug Store to read them. Finding ice cream chairs to sit on. An empty table, so that we could sit together. Maybe ordering a float or a milk shake. Vanilla and strawberry are my favourite kinds.

When we got to be teenagers, we went to the record store. The songs would be playing as we walked in the door. We would be going through the great stack of records. Looking for a tune that might be on the Hit Parade. The records had brown papers on them so they wouldn't get scratched. My first record I ever bought was "Hey There", by Rosemary Clooney. We played our records over and over, but never trading them. We would take them to Joanie Bond's house on Stanley Street, and play them in her den with the red leather couches. That's where her record player was. "ShBoom" was the song we danced to there, the most. ShBoom always reminded me of Joanie's house. The records, prized possessions.

Ringing in the New Year

Judy's family do something special every New Year's Eve. They go outside with their pots and pans and make noise to ring in the New Year. I can hear them when they do it, living just across the street. I have wanted and wanted to do it but I was never allowed. Not until I was older. I finally got to be a part of it. Judy's mother gives Judy, Donnie and me a pot and cover to bang. We take our places out on the veranda. Standing close to each other to be really loud. There is no one else around that I can see or hear. Cold and still, the snow looking pretty. We clang and clang them. Me, dropping the pot lid. An awful lot of racket coming from just us! I wonder if we are waking people up. I feel kind of silly doing it. But it is fun! When it is just past midnight, I have to go home and go to bed.

Famous Folks

We hear we have a famous family living in North Sydney. Their house is behind the Odeon Theatre. A nice sized house with a veranda. We pass it quite often and comment. Could it be true or not true? The gentleman who owns the house is a doctor. Dr. MacLean. We have never seen Dr. MacLean or his wife. No one ever sitting out. Quite, quiet, really. Dr. MacLean's daughter teaches students at Acadia University in Wolfville, Nova Scotia. She has famous children, Shirley MacLaine and Warren Beatty. We see them on the screen at the show. It's like we know them personally. Like they are a part of us. Like they are from North Sydney! Judy and I loved "Splendor in the Grass." Warren is so dreamy. I think they may visit here sometimes. People say they do. We keep looking for them and hoping.

Snow Forts

Judy and I have great fun in snow banks. Since we were eight, nine and ten. We like to climb up them. Being careful not to fall below on the street in the way of the cars. The snow falling around us. We can see their bright lights going back and forth. Looking so pretty. We are standing way up high and looking all around. I feel like a giant up here! Snow drifts blowing. Up and down we go. We dig our holes. Digging them out with our mittens. It isn't an easy thing to be doing. Our mittens soon getting wet and soggy. Our fingers cold and freezing. It's kind of like being in an igloo in here. A bit dark, but quite cozy. We are shivering but we don't want to come in yet. Just sitting and talking. In no time at all, I have to go to the bathroom. I don't want to go in. I am trying to hold it. Really hard. Trying not to think about it. Then, I do it. I pee my pants! My pants are feeling warm. I don't tell Judy. I am suddenly feeling very cold and wet in my pants. Not too great a feeling. I have to go home. Judy doesn't want to. My peeing ruined my time. I wasn't allowed to play out anymore. Judy had to go home. I had to get on my pyjamas. I have decided that I am not going to wet my pants again.

Judy and I had a fight once because she said something I didn't like. I put her head in a snow bank! It was fun for me. She was crying and crying. She ran to my house to tell my mother. I was in trouble! It was all her fault! I didn't put her head in a snow bank again, ever.

Home Remedies

Aunt Grace was known to some for her healing powers. Namely removing warts. Shirley had warts all over her hands. My mother called Aunt Grace and asked if she could come and take them off. Shirley was told not to mention the warts at all when Aunt Grace came to the house. It wouldn't work if she did. Aunt Grace was waiting when Shirley came home from school. Aunt Grace was finishing her tea. I was watching. My mother gave Aunt Grace a small piece of red, raw meat. She took Shirley's hands and rubbed the meat all over them. There was no talking going on. She was just rubbing. Soon after Aunt Grace went home. My mother buried the piece of meat in the back yard. In a couple of days, Shirley's warts were gone. Like magic! When I was four, I had a wart under my knee. My Uncle Tom spotted it, tied a long piece of thread around it in a knot and tied the other end to an open door. When he shut the door the wart came out roots and all. There is nothing to describe it! I thought I was going to faint.

The Basket Lady

A lady would come to our house in the spring and fall selling her baskets. She came from Eskasoni. She had many, many baskets all colours, sizes and shapes. She would arrive early in the morning when Shirley and I were going to school, and still be there at lunch time. She would just be leaving when I got home from school in the afternoon. My mother didn't need any more of her baskets. She felt she had to buy something from her. She didn't want to hurt the lady's feelings.

A pastime for the ladies was having their fortunes told with tea leaves. If we kids were around, we had our tea leaves done, too. Not a drop of tea could be left in the teacup for the reading.

Mixed Parties

When you became a teenager, mixed parties were allowed. Always chaperoned of course, by the parents. Birthday parties were a really big thing. You felt really left out if you weren't invited to one. Judy talked me into going to a party house uninvited. We looked through the window to see who was there, who was invited, and what they were doing. The party person came out and asked us to go away. Embarrassing a bit, to say the least, but we didn't care. We didn't invite her to our parties.

Popular games were Spin the Bottle and Post Office. I can remember being in a closet kissing a boy and we purposely stayed and stayed, making everyone think we were doing something we shouldn't be doing. Sometimes you would be in there with someone you didn't want to be in there with. That visit to the closet was a really quick one. The girls would be whispering and giggling about the kissing and who was the best. Everyone would be waiting on the other side of the door wondering what was going on. Someone would open the door and then the next person would spin. We always kissed with our lips closed. Then came French kissing! Feeling the boy's tongue. Yuck! We always wanted to be older. Thirteen, sixteen, eighteen, twenty-one. When we got there we felt the same as we always had.

We dreamed of getting married, what our husbands would look like. The colour of his eyes and hair very important. What our wedding dresses might be like? We love to sing and hum, "Here Comes the Bride." Our version was "Here Comes the Bride, Short, Fat and Wide." We would see so many brides in their gowns at the weddings we sang at. We'd be dreaming! It was not unusual to sneak into the back row of the church and watch a wedding going on. Let's say the wedding parties always had a lot of guests and no one noticing us.

Judy dances and dances. So does Donnie. You should see them dancing together. The advantage Judy has over me is knowing the boys who are Donnie's friends. To die for! She meets the boys first. She knows how to dance with them and she knows what to say. I just stand there with my mouth hanging open.

The Spelling Bee

I remember one year there was a Spelling Bee at Thompson High. There was some anticipation. I liked to spell, maybe that's why. We all had to hone up on our words. Practicing with each other. Not knowing what words we were going to be asked. We all gathered in the gymnasium. Everyone was nervous and waiting for their turn. It seemed we were always waiting for something. We filed on stage one after the other. It took some time before we were down to a handful. I was the first runner up. I can't remember the word I missed. I remember David won. He was in the contest from the beginning. Competing and competing. Afterwards, I couldn't believe that I missed the word I was given. It wasn't very hard. I felt pretty stupid. For a day anyway!

Youth Groups

Flo Hare is the lovely lady who is in charge of most of the activities at our church. She is married and has children of her own. Her husband Lloyd, supports her in her many things. You always see Flo walking up to the parish hall. She is in charge of the Junior Auxiliary, Girl's Auxiliary, and AYPA. Groups. She is also a member of the Evening Branch and Women's Auxiliary and the Altar Guild. Where she got the time to do it all I don't know! She makes our growing up years so much fun. We loved playing musical chairs and marching to "The Grand Old Duke of York" in JA and GA. As hard as she tried to teach me, I still had holes in my knitting. In AYPA, we get to socialize with the boys and we get to dance. "Peggy Sue", sung by Buddy Holly, was a favourite song to dance to. Everyone singing, "Peggy Sue, Peggy Sue, Pretty, Pretty, Pretty, Pretty,

Peggy Sue" as they danced. The song is great! Practicing our steps for the high school dances. Flo is a wonderful friend to all of us. Flo gives so many hours of her time to us kids at St. Johns' Church and the congregation. No one else gave of their time like Flo did. Maybe, only my father!

Prank Calls and Other Antics

One evening, when no one was home, Judy came over to keep me company. What did we find ourselves doing? We were using the telephone. Calling boys and hanging up. Changing our voices so that no one would know who we were. The phone cord would be all curled up. Being nervous on the telephone and twirling and twirling it. One of our favourite past times! My telephone was always ringing and so was everybody else's. Lots of busy telephone lines. Party lines, too. Don't forget to call so and so was a familiar saying. At school, we would compare notes to see who had been on the phone the longest. Ethel had been on the telephone for seven hours with a boy from Sydney Mines. ONE CALL! We couldn't believe it! No one could top that!

One night, Judy and Joan Peters came over. My parents were out. Judy was in the bathroom using our bathroom sink. The telephone rang. I answered and it was for her. I yelled up the call is for you. I knew Judy picked it up. No one liked anyone listening in to a boy and girl call. Hushed voices were used. To make it romantic, I guess. It didn't seem as if too much time had passed when I heard water running. Really running! I ran around trying to find out where the water was coming from. Lo and behold, water was coming through the living room ceiling without letting up. Dripping like Niagara Falls all over my mother's piano. I screamed up to Judy and Joan, "there's water running!" They were none the wiser. I hightailed it to the top of the stairs. Water all over the bathroom floor. Judy had left the plug in the sink with the water running. Too intent on her telephone call to even think about having done it. We all figured we were in for it! What to do? We were waiting for the shit to hit the fan! When my Mum and Dad came home.

Surprisingly, not very much was said at all. Maybe, it was because my friends were there. The next day a man came in to fix the ceiling. Mum's piano was alright. Were we relieved! Our not feeling so guilty about it then.

Going for a Spin

Judy and I spend a lot of time in my Uncle Tom's red, hard top, "Oldsmobile Holiday" convertible. It is parked in our garage for the winter. Gaultois has no roads so Uncle Tom keeps it there for his trips to Montreal. It has automatic windows. We had never seen automatic windows before. It is fun pushing on the buttons to make them go up and down. We feel very grown up turning on the key and listening to the tunes on the CBC and CJCB in Sydney. "Ship to Shore Melodies", we would listen to on a Saturday night. Bob Bambury, from North Sydney, is the announcer. Also, listening to "The Hit Parade" on Sunday afternoons. We can't leave the key on too long or the battery will go dead. We take our turns at the wheel. The whole time staying stationary. Until one Sunday night, being very daring, and the coast clear, I started the engine, garage doors open, we inched out very slowly. We gained speed after a few blocks. I didn't have a driver's licence, Judy didn't either. Oh, was it daring and exciting! We are fifteen at the time. As we passed our church, one of the church wardens saw us go by. Fortunately, he didn't squeal on us! My father never found out.

I always love washing the "Oldsmobile" and our black 1953 "Dodge". I love both cars. Dad liked his squeaky clean with no streaks. I loved to study in our driveway sitting in the front seat. Talking to any friends going by. Cars are a big thing with me. I want to be a motor mechanic, maybe. I like identifying them, the car styles are so different. Cars are also a great place for parking. On the dirt roads, in front of your house. Judy and I are full of badness!

Beauty Secrets

We like the days of the week underwear. We girls all have to have a package of them. Lifting up our skirts to show them off. Monday, Tuesday, Wednesday etc. False fingernails that you can glue on top of your own. The nails are very tricky to be putting on. They look much pointier than your own finger nails. You have to cut around them with the scissors. A finger nail file just doesn't do it. They don't always look the way they should be looking. A coat of natural polish to make them look shiny. They look witchy if you paint them red. They get in the way when you want to be doing something like using the telephone or going to the bathroom! You might lose one or they may fall off.

Noxzema for the pimples. You can tell if someone is using it when they walk by, the strong whiff it lets off. A favourite pastime, pinching someone else's pimples with your fingers or with a bobby pin! A beauty secret! An egg yolk beaten up and applied to your face until it gets dried up and cracky. To the sink for a quick rinse. Was it gucky!! Now the egg white patted on and left until your face is feeling tight. Sitting very still so it won't crack. Your face soon feels very tight! Do I mean tight? Rinsing again. When you look in the mirror, your face is squeaky clean.

Home Economics

In High School, a new subject is Home Economics. We learned to cook things on a very small scale. I remember we made an eighth of a chocolate cake and made boiled icing. It was delicious but it certainly didn't make us fat. We were given a sheet of the Canada Food Rules and had to remember so many servings of what to eat each day. The other part of the class was sewing. Let's put it this way. I didn't like the sewing part. It was my first attempt. Everyone had to make a white apron. A dress or blouse and skirt for the School Fashion show. Grades 9 - 12 girls all had to do it. We all went downtown to get our supplies. Choosing the pattern from the Simplicity, Butterick or McCall books. There were so many patterns to choose from. Your head would be in a tizzy! Then looking for the material. What kind to buy? The thread to match. It felt good when you had it all in the bag to take home. I picked out a dress pattern with a peter pan collar. A flowered, polished, cotton material. Cutting the pieces out at school was something else again. Putting down the tissue paper and pinning it on top of the material. Needing help from the teacher if the tissue paper ran over it. I would sew and rip out, sew and rip out. Then it would be the pressing and the ironing. We worked on our things for at least two months. I was so sick of looking at the dreaded dress. You could see all of the holes where I had ripped it out. The dress looked terrible to me, by the time it was finished.

We all strutted our stuff in the fashion show doing our twirls. One step with the right foot, one step with the left and twirl. The teacher had us practice them until we got our steps right. On the big night of the Fashion Show, the mothers were in the gymnasium watching. Some of them taking pictures. They were proud of their daughter's sewing achievements. Pleased about how they looked. I still have a picture of me in my dreaded dress. When I went home, I dumped the dress in the garbage can without anyone knowing. I never wanted to see it again. Some of the girls wore theirs for a long time. Their dresses looked much better than mine!

Glamour Girls

Thompson High friends. Allie Jean (second from right)

We girls go to Stedmans for our beauty supplies. We don't wear a lot of makeup but we do our thing. Lipstick is very important. I call it lips!! We blot it on a Kleenex if we apply too much. We kiss a boy's cheek to leave lip marks. I can't forget hickies on the neck. The unmentionables! They are quickly covered up with a collar. Do the girls blush if they are seen? It is a really big thing when the frosted look came in. For the lips, I mean. White lipstick on top of a red or pink one. We have eye lash curlers, eyebrow pencils, compacts compete with puffs. Opening and shutting them. Opening and shutting them. Looking in and looking in. Trying out the puff. You never get tired of looking! It seems you are always cleaning the mirror. Then someone wants to be borrowing it. A small amount of rouge on top of the foundation. Powder completes the look. Glamorous! Like Doris Day in the movies. Hair pins are a must for the girls who have French rolls. Brush rollers and picks the girls use a lot for teasing. Hair clips for setting the kiss curls. Having bangs and page boys are popular hair styles too. A little dab of perfume behind the ears is a must. We can all afford to use Evening in Paris cologne. Our mothers buy Evening in Paris, perfume. Lorna is one of our friends at Thompson High. She is the only girl we know who keeps a diary faithfully. She would always be rushing home after school to make an entry. We never knew about who or what. She was very secretive about it. When we visited Lorna's bedroom we would see the diary complete with lock, but no one, not anyone, could have a peek! I remember getting a diary, but never got past January in the writing. Diaries are the in thing for a while. Much like our ankle bracelets. If you wear the bracelet on the left leg you are going steady. On the right leg you are available. Your first pair of pumps is a very big occasion. You feel so grown up strutting in them. Judy wears her ankle socks in hers!

The Hair Salon and Home Perms

Kiss curl hairdos done with bobby pins. You could go to the hairdresser and have a shampoo, cut and set for $1.00. I had a Newfie perm one spring. My hair was so frizzy and out of control. I pestered my mother to take me back and have it cut off. Needless to say, she wasn't too pleased. I just wasn't going to let any one of my friends see me looking like that! The hairdresser put hot curlers on my head. Before too long, I felt a burning sensation on the top of my head. The next thing I knew, the hairdresser poured cold water over my head! I was sizzling!! And soaked!! You felt uneasy going to the hairdresser's much like you do when you went to the dentist's office. Fear of facing the drill or your mouth frozen for ages. Some of the girls and mothers would give each other Toni permanents. The Toni came in a small box with little pink rollers, setting lotion and little white papers. What a smell it made! Stinging your eyes like you wouldn't believe! The lotion running down your neck and onto your clothes. Sometimes you would have to give the Toni twice to get some curls to appear. What a thing to get the rollers to close when your hair was sitting in them! Everyone wanting to try it. It was a cheap way to get a perm.

"Fresh Fish"

An embarrassing time was in the 10th grade. I had to have my front tooth pulled. I had to go to school like that for TEN days!! Waiting for my false plate to come in. A gaping HOLE! I was known as Gummer by Ralph in my class. I remember kids asking me to say "fresh fish" and "fresh fruit." I was MORTIFIED! It wasn't a good time to say the least.

Driving Around Town

It was a big deal to get your father's car and take your friends for a ride. When this happened, you had more friends than you knew youhad! It wasn't unusual to have everyone chip in for the gas. One dollar would usually do it. Sometimes, when the boys didn't have any money, they would siphon gas from someone's car. The car owner none the wiser. If the gas gauge was really low coming home, you would be sure to top it up a bit. The gas needle looking like it was in the same place as when you started out. The rear view mirror for checking out the lipstick and hairdo's. As a rule, a firm one, the ashtrays had to be emptied before returning home. No tell tale signs of smoking, going on! We drive to Upper North Sydney for our gas. Adam or Roy LeMoine would be working. We would have our visit with them and then take off again. The Mountie station nearby. Many a time, a Mountie would ride your bumper. Trying to get you to go over the speed limit. This happened most times with the boys. Did the Mounties think they were hot! "Lewie" Clark, Mr. Carter and Mr. Meaney were our policemen. I should say "Lewie" Clark was the chief of police. The policemen would always be around town, chatting to people as they went by. Checking door ways and making sure everything was alright. We didn't have any crime, to speak of, in North Sydney. It was usually very quiet. Judy knew "Lewie" Clark personally. She would say they were related. She told everyone she knew. Having the same last name as his and all. I never believed it!

Our Teacher "Jeep"

Judy and I meet our friends at the stone wall in front of our math teacher's house. We would sit there for hours it seemed shooting the breeze after supper. The friends would be gathering all night long. One time, Miss MacDonald, Jeep to us, had a man put manure on the other side of the wall to keep us from sitting. Needless to say, we didn't notice it or smell it at all! We were just doing our thing. Sitting, talking and looking. Hoping, someone special would come by. Miss MacDonald is my very favourite teacher in high school. She has a wonderful figure. The boys always watch her as she leaves the classroom. Hubba, hubba ding dings! Every spring and fall she buys her new wardrobes. She wears skirts mostly and long-sleeved cardigans. Sometimes wearing them back to front. She pushes her sleeves up to her elbows. We girls do it, too. Miss MacDonald likes to horse around with the boys in her different classes. Hitting them over their heads with her math book. Even throwing chalk at them if they are acting up. The guys like getting a charge out of her. She is a lot of fun! She is an excellent teacher! I guess Jeep is the reason why I like math so much. Her easy going manner and sense of fun.

The Soda Shop

Our favourite haunts are Ivey's and Hare's. The hours we spend! Dancing at Ivey's to the jukebox. Sitting on stools having our chips and gravy, hamburgers and cherry cokes. Being asked to dance by buddy Andrea is a thrill. A nickel buys two cigarettes and a bubble gum. The kids are always a coming and a going. You always make a point of noticing who might come through the front screen door. Jiving with a girlfriend to see if anyone will notice and ask you to dance. Our place to socialize and meet your heart throb. You find us there after school and after supper. Pinball machines are all along one wall. Do the boys shake those machines with the flippers going. The points adding up as the game goes on. The lights going on and off. The ding dinging. The excitement to win a free game. The girls try it too, but the boys are better at it. Joan

Hare has a big picture window in front of her shop. That's where the boys park their cars. You can see everything going on outside. If a certain someone is striding in, you have a little time to fix your lipstick. Max Factor, of course.

There is always the wondering about who might show up that night. The guys talking to each other and maybe slicking back their hair. You can usually see a black comb in a back pocket. The girls giggling and poking each other in the ribs. We can't dance at Hare's, not enough room. There are booths for seating and tiny jukeboxes at each table. The music never stops. A serving counter and the cooking done at the back. Joan serves fries and hamburgers, along with fish and chips. We all wait to be served. It isn't unusual to be sprinkling the salt and pepper shakers on the table and making a great mess. Ashtrays, soon overflowing. Smoking is a very in thing to be doing. Everyone trying it at least once. Trying to blow smoke rings like the boys is a big feat. Matinee cigarettes the girls like and Export A with the cork tips. The boys like Export plain. The Iveys and Joan put up with the loud music, the talking and all the goings on. They must have the patience of Job. They are very nice people.

Josie's at Leitche's Creek

In the summer we go to Josie's in Leitche's Creek. It started out as an outdoor snack bar, but later on Josie added a dining room. Josie serves the best hamburgers and hot sandwiches anywhere. Her food has a very special taste. The smell when you walk in is something else again. The best gravy. To die for! Ice cream in cones over the counter or served inside. 5 cents for a single and 10 cents for a double. We go to Wong's on Commercial Street for Chinese food. Their egg rolls have meat and vegetables. Sometimes the chopsticks don't work quite right. Trying to manipulate them with your fingers. You look and feel quite clumsy if you have a boy sitting across from you. You trying your best to look sophisticated. We look forward to reading each other's fortune cookies.

Our Magazines

The "Cape Breton Post", "The Chronicle Herald" and "The Star Weekly" are our newspapers. Our parents like them all. We girls like to read "Modern Screen", "Screenplay" and "Photoplay" magazines. We read all about our favourite movie stars over and over again. The coloured pictures are always so nice to look at. We cut them out and hang them on our bedroom walls and swoon over the movie stars. Dorothy Cameron has such a big stack of movie magazines in her bedroom. To die for! Lucky for me, she gives me her old ones when she gets tired of them. I am thrilled about that. She always has new ones that she hasn't read yet. "True Confessions" and "Modern Romance" are popular with some of the mothers. Girls would try and sneak them when there was no one else around. There is lots of hugging and kissing going on in the pictures. We are trying to find out about the birds and the bees!

The best fashion magazine is "Seventeen". We would be dreaming about and wishing for the lovely clothes. You wanted them all! The looking and wishing was about it. The clothes were all so expensive and came from the United States. The Simpson's catalogue everybody had at their house. You could order anything you wanted. Sometimes the item didn't look anything like it did in the catalogue, when it came into the store. Then back to looking again and reordering or not bothering.

National Geographic we see copies of at school. The boys are really drawn to some of the pages! My father had a subscription to Reader's Digest that he subscribed to every year. In the fall, Thompson High and "MacLean's Magazine" would have a contest selling magazine subscriptions. We kids would go door to door eagerly selling them at first. Everyone would be running all over the place. Hitting every door in sight. Our order forms and pens in hand. Out of breath, when you made it to a door. Then trying to look natural when someone answered. Not really knowing what to say about the magazines. A house could be hit three or four times. We were all so determined to get an order. The fun of it, soon wore off.

It wasn't easy selling magazines. You didn't like to hear someone at the door saying, "No, I don't want any. Don't come back again!" I would take it personally. It made me feel bad and very stupid. There were three prizes for the students who sold the most subscriptions. One year I won a "Kodak" brownie camera. I couldn't believe it. I didn't think I had sold that many subscriptions. It was quite a thing to be a winner. The first thing I had ever won. I had my Kodak camera for a long time. I didn't sell any more subscriptions after that. Selling them wasn't as much fun as I thought it would be!

Norma Jean

When Judy was sixteen, she got a baby sister. Was I surprised! Donnie called me from the hospital to tell me. He and Judy were there seeing her for the first time. At first, I didn't understand what he was talking about. He kept saying it and then it finally sunk in. A baby sister! I got a bit of a clue I guess, thinking about it now. When I came home from Judy's house one time, my mother asked if Mrs. Clark might be in the "family way." I didn't know what she meant. I remember saying, "No, Mum." Like what a funny thing to be asking. I forgot all about it.

Norma Jean was born on April 13, 1956. Norma was given my middle name. Was I proud! She was so tiny coming home. Judy and I got to do lots of baby-sitting. We took our turns. She was like our very own baby. When she could talk she called me "wawie." She called Judy, "my Judy." She has lots of fun with the kids coming and going to the Clark's house. Everybody loves Norma Jean.

The Postal Clerk

We also go to the Riverview High School Dances in Coxheath and the Y dances in Sydney. The "Acadians" played at the Y. An excellent live brass band. They play all of our favourite tunes. Even the songs from the "Hit Parade". They also played at the New Year's Ball. Our friendships expanded to Coxheath and Sydney with the dances. The North Sydney boys didn't like us dating anyone else but them. Sometimes a fight would break out because someone was jealous of someone else. Invading their territory so to speak! It was rather childish. But we girls felt flattered!

I met a boy at the Y who went to Sydney Academy. He worked part time at the Post Office. It was a great thrill to receive letters in my mailbox and especially from a boy. But in this case, Special Delivery letters, love letters from him. I felt very special. I had never received a Special Delivery letter before. I shared them with Judy. We would go to the Post Office every day after school and check out our box number

352. You could see right in the glass door. If I didn't have the key I would have to ask the Postmaster, Mr. Penny, and was he pleased, not at all! The excitement generated when there was something in the box. We looked at them together and shared. The only time I saw the Sydney boy was at the Y dance. I would get great letters saying he would see me at the dance. Most of the time he wouldn't ask me to dance at all, or ask to take me home. I would go and be totally ignored by him. I found out later that he wrote many girls and pulled the same thing. The letter bit! The "ignoring" us at dance routine. It was interesting to say the least and puzzling. He probably wanted all of us to love him madly. Everyone wanting him type of thing. He was not doing. Not for us anyway.

Bernadine and Fun & Games

If we aren't out driving, we're in Judy's living room. The record player always playing. The song "Bernadine" we listened to over and over. Judy's little sister Norma thought that that was what the record player was called. Bernadine! Norma Jean is about two and half at the time. She is always talking and pointing to Bernadine. Donnie, Judy and I take turns dancing. Donnie teaches us to slow dance, and jive. He is a great dancer. The room is jumping! Especially, when Donnie is in his room playing his drums. Judy and I racing up and down the stairs.

Answering and making telephone calls. The ringing never stops. The telephone would be passed back and forth and the same gossip would be repeated. Making a date to meet at someone's house or meeting at a hamburger shop. Often, we played Canasta at the Clark's kitchen table. Judy's mum and dad teaching us. The game would never end it seemed. Then we would play again. Was it fun!

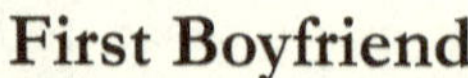

First Boyfriend

John and Allie Jean, prom photo

John is my boyfriend. He lives on Pierce Street, just up from Thompson High and Ivey's. John and I met at the Odeon Theatre. We did know each other a little bit when we were in the Junior Choir. When we weren't thinking of each other as girl and boy. John and his buddies were sitting behind Judy and me at the show. John was fooling around, putting his scarf around my neck. Pulling it back and forth being silly! What you would call flirting. We all started laughing. After the movie, we all walked home together for a ways. John asks me if I would like to go out with him sometime. I said "Okay", blushing. Not too long after, we were going steady. You didn't go out with any other boy or even look at another boy after that. John and I went out together or with his friends or mine. Going to John's house is a fun thing to be doing.

John's mother has an open house, so to speak, for his friends and any of mine who want to come there. We are always welcome to visit and hang out. We shoot the breeze and watch television. We even skip school there to watch the World Series. The New York Yankees are the team we root for. I like Joe DiMaggio and Mickey Mantle. We feel comfortable, relaxed and grown up having our cigarettes at John's. John's mother tells us if any ashes fall on the rug not to worry. She doesn't mind. It is good for the moths. She is so good to us!

Driving Test

Your sixteenth birthday! Time to try for your driver's test. The driver's manual is read from cover to cover, falling apart. A great uneasiness as you get in your father's car with the inspector. Not much talking going on, on his part. He had his papers and pen in place. A gruff, "pull out", to me. Looking over my left shoulder I inch out. A "right turn here", "park there", "back up there", "stop at the stop signs", over and over. My knuckles tight on the wheel and feeling like my stomach is going to burst. Am I going to pass? No clue from him. The test is suddenly, surprisingly, over. I get the news! I didn't stop long enough at a stop sign! The stop sign right in front of my house. Am I disappointed! The next try I passed. Then, everyone wanted a ride! What a thrill it was to get it! Everybody wanted to be your friend!

The New Teachers

In Grade 10 we have two new teachers. The school is a buzz. The girls excited! Probably because the teachers are so young and very good-looking. Everyone wanting to be talking to them. To be noticed! Any excuse to be doing it! They like to kid around with us. They aren't that much older than we kids are. Mr. Wayne from Glace Bay and Mr. Gardener from Sydney Mines. Mr. Gardener is my home room teacher. He teaches us History. I work so hard on my English monarchs. All the kings and queens. Trying to keep them all straight in my mind. Maybe, because, it was for Mr. Gardener. I managed to get 92 per cent on my paper. A $2.00 prize even.

The Angel

There is a special girl at Thompson High School. She has the lightest, finest, blond hair of anyone. She has a pale complexion and her cheeks get really really pink, almost red, when she blushes. She puts her hands up to her face in embarrassment when she does it. She's probably thinking we are all looking at her, and we are! She looks so beautiful. Not only beautiful on the outside but on the inside too. Her name is Adrienne Angel and her name suits her to a tee. Adrienne is a friend to everyone, including me.

Assemblies

In high school we have assembly on Friday mornings. A chance to miss a regular class. Everybody likes the assemblies. The announcements are made by the principal, Mr. Kenney. Following the announcements, the talented students get to perform. Playing their violins, singing a current song, playing their piano pieces or reciting poetry. The entertainment seems to be the same variety each week. Adrienne Angel and June Groves playing the piano. Normie Johnson, Jean and Sandy Allen, the twins, always playing their violins. Mr. Allen is always waiting backstage to take their violins home. John Edmunds playing his harmonica and doing a comedy routine. George McNeil plays his fiddle. You didn't see Judy and me on center stage. I guess you can say we aren't too great in the talent department. We certainly have tried! One assembly, a man came and played his very expensive violin. A Stradivarius or something that sounds like that. The violin looked just the same as an ordinary one. He was very careful handling it. He told us everything there was to be knowing about the violin.

School Dances

Judy and I really like the school dances. We have about five dances a year. It is quite a thing to be asked to be on the decorating committee. A bunch of us make posters with bristol board that we tack up all over the school walls to advertise. We twirl the crepe paper and hang them in the gymnasium. Lots and lots of them. We have a Sadie Hawkins dance too, the girls inviting the boys. You are sure of a date for that dance. You can keep asking until you get one. Some of the girls are too shy to ask a boy. It usually works out alright in the end.

The Most Popular Girl and Boy Dance is one we look forward to the most. Everyone votes for their most favourite girl and boy at Thompson High School. The names are announced in the classrooms before the dance. The formal announcement is made at the dance. The Most Popular girl and Most Popular boy have a dance. Catherine Beaton and Murdock Morrison win.

Everyone is cheering and yelling for them. Happy for the winning decision. Catherine and Murdock get to dance together on the dance floor by themselves. We are all watching them and the next song we all

get to join in on. The other dances are regular ones, with the Prom in June. The teachers taking turns chaperoning the dances along with some of the student's parents. There are chairs placed all around the auditorium. The girls are sitting and waiting, impatiently waiting, for someone to ask them to dance. Maybe waiting for someone special to come along. It isn't unusual to see the girls dancing with each other. The girls are the best dancers for the most part.

We are always practicing with each other. Even at the dance! There are some guys you really would like to dance with. Maybe not as a date but for their dancing capabilities. "Jiving" is our thing! "Slow dancing," a romantic thing! Especially, if you are dancing with your boyfriend or someone you might be interested in. At the beginning of the dance, a lot of the guys have cold feet. Numerous times, someone might ask a girl and they definitely might not be interested. The girl thinking I don't want to dance with him. Maybe he's too short. Maybe he's too shy. Maybe he has two left feet. I can never refuse anyone. I don't want them to feel bad. Some girls do refuse and the boys look so downcast and embarrassed. They take forever to ask anyone again.

We have a record player and our favourite tunes are playing. Maybe it's a song reminding you of a particular person, a place, a particular happening in your life. We all swoon to the music. I like "Blueberry Hill", "It's All in the Game", "Twilight Time", "The Great Pretender", "Don't Be Cruel", "Splish Splash", "Mack the Knife", "Smoke Gets in Your Eyes", "Lucille", "Mona Lisa", "The Twelfth of Never", "Are You Lonesome Tonight?", "ShBoom", "Memories are Made of This", "Love Letters in the Sand", "Cherry Pink and Apple Blossom White", "Chances Are", "Who's Sorry Now?", "Donna", "Sincerely", "In the Still of the Night". The last song they play at the Riverview High dances on a Saturday night is always "The Twelfth of Never" by Johnny Mathis. The song is so romantic!

Discovering Elvis

We saw Elvis first, when he appeared for the first time on "The Tommy Dorsey Show", and "The Ed Sullivan Show". Everybody watching Ed Sullivan every Sunday night at eight o'clock. My mother likes Elvis' singing and the fact that he wiggles. My mother's favourite Elvis song is "When My Blue Moon Turns to Gold Again." Two of our school chums, Joan Salter and Peggy Day start an Elvis Fan club. They go all over the school asking if anyone wants to join. Elvis is our heart throb! Who doesn't like "Blue Suede Shoes" and "I Want You, I Need You, I Love You?" We all lined up for his movie "Love Me Tender". We never thought the doors would open fast enough. We were all so excited to be seeing him like almost in person. Like Warren! All of us so anxious to get in. The girls so giddy! The movie starts with Elvis standing in a field. I melt when I see him!! Do we cheer! When the movie is over, we are all in tears. Elvis dies in the movie. Not long after that, some of the boys start sporting ducktails and long side burns, to be cool like Elvis. Black leather jackets even. Even trying to talk and move like he does. A great stride to their walking all of a sudden.

The Prom

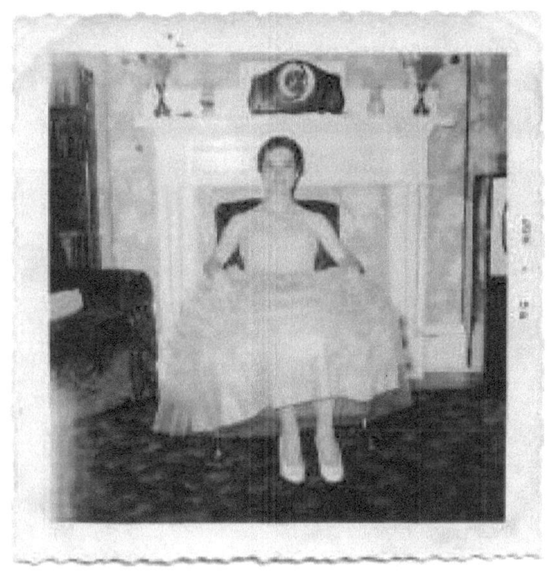

Allie Jean waiting for her prom date

When the prom is announced, there is the mounting anticipation. Am I going to be asked? Nervous and nervous about it!! Will he? Won't he? Being asked, very relieved, and then the big question, "What am I going to wear?" There is something very grown up about going to your first formal dance. Making us girls feel tingly and Cinderellaish! There are two ladies stores in North Sydney. Bond's Ladies Wear and Balah's. You can also go to the Smart Shop and other ladies stores in Sydney if you can't find a dress in North Sydney. My mother comes with me to find my gown. Am I excited and worried I won't find the right one. A blue, strapless, three-tiered net long dress we find, right away. The dress costs $29.95. Expensive! The dress is so beautiful!

My Aunt Laura happens to be visiting at Prom time. Aunt Laura helps me to get ready. Mum is watching the goings on and very excited for me. I was feeling so nervous about it all! It was the first time I ever had my eyebrows plucked. Aunt Laura pulled them out one by one. Did it hurt! She told me if you put perfume on top of your lipstick, the lipstick would stay on longer. It works!

Your date asks beforehand what the colour of your dress will be, so he can buy a matching corsage. Meeting your parents goes along with the evening. Your date has to come into the living room, let's say for inspection! My parents checking the boy out. We are in a hurry to leave, after the third degree. When he has to have you home etc. Promising to be home at the appointed hour. We are both fluttery and nervous and wanting to leave in a hurry!

Friends, Allie Jean (second from right) and John

When you arrive at the school gymnasium everyone is very excited and bubbly. Everybody twirling around looking at each other's gowns. The gowns swishing as we jive. Our crinolines making them stick out so much and getting in the way of our dancing. The dresses are every colour of the rainbow! Some are strapless and others with spaghetti straps and some with jackets. Strapless dresses are very daring for us to be wearing. The boys dolled up in their suits, white shirts and ties. Sporting their cuff links and a carnation in their lapels. Everybody is looking very fancy! The girls, maybe wearing more lipstick than usual. Perfume behind their ears. Earrings and necklaces, looking very nice. Some girls have stardust in their hair to make your hair look glittery and pretty. The hairdresser puts it on if you ask her to. The stardust costs a dollar extra. We talk, laugh, giggle and change partners galore. What fun we are having!!

John brings me a pink and white carnation, dress corsage. I see the other girls with red, white or pink carnations. Other corsages made up with baby, white roses. Beautiful, wrist corsages as well. The dress corsage gets crushed if you are dancing too close to your date. Some girls prefer the wrist ones for that reason. When I get home, I plan to put my corsage in the refrigerator for saving. A souvenir for my scrapbook or between the pages of a book.

Friends, Alice (second from right) and John

After the prom, we all head out to the Silver Rail on the Sydney highway. A very, nice, supper club place with a dance floor. Tables and booths all around the huge room. Do we feel grown up there being out on the town with our friends? No parents around to spy on us! We are away from North Sydney. A big night out on the town for us! We are having our "freedom". We dance to the songs on the jukebox. There is no drinking allowed. We don't do that anyway. A lot of us do smoke. This is our big sin! The girls in their gowns and the boys looking so handsome. A very different look at school.

Coming into the Silver Rail is a very special thing. Different couples spotting you and wanting you to sit with them. The waving and compliments as you walk by. Maybe sitting at the next table, if theirs is filled. How we jive and slow dance! Everybody strutting their stuff! Before too long, we order a hot chicken, hot hamburger or hot beef sandwich with fries, gravy and peas. Cherry cokes we all have. We dance, while we wait for our meals to be served. Then back to the dancing after we have eaten. Changing partners, over and over again. Jiving and jiving!! Until you are so out of breath you have to quit! Our going outside for a little fresh air, and a kiss is a natural thing to be doing! We are all very talkative and silly.

The boys have their father's cars for the evening. Two couples may go in one car or one couple on their own. We arrive home just before one o'clock in the morning. To keep the curfew! It is a very late night for me. Midnight, being curfew for an ordinary dance. Going parking is a given, before you head home. You look quite rumpled when you land on your doorstep. Lipstick smeared! Hair askew! Magic night!

(Ten years later, the Silver Rail was destroyed by fire. A lot of memories went with the restaurant. Not only for the Thompson High students but the high school students from the nearby towns who went there for their Prom nights too). It was a fun place to be!

Exams

Exam time! Worry and worry. Studying and cramming. Not fit to talk to. Will the teachers ask the right questions? Looking out the window, trying to come up with an answer. Watching the clock to see if there is enough time to finish the exam. The classroom, hot, on June days. Complete silence. Messing up your foolscap and feeling too embarrassed to ask for another piece. The teacher walking slowly up and down the aisles. Stopping here and there while you write. Making you feel nervous. The long-awaited bell finally rings! Everyone out the door in a flash! So relieved the exam is over! The great dread, comparing answers in the hallway. Soon, finding out your answers may not be right. Back to the books, to do it again, tomorrow!!

Lockers

What a great thing you think it is, having your own locker in high school. We didn't have them at Central School. Combination and pad locks. What fun, but not really! Especially, if you forget the combination numbers or lose your key! Binders and scribblers tumbling off the top shelves. Movie stars pasted inside the locker doors. A meeting place, between classes to shoot the breeze with your friends for a few minutes. Students and teachers whizzing by to get to the next class. Always lots of chatter and giggling going on. Maybe some whispering about who is skipping school that day! Hiding something in someone else's locker, you don't want anyone else to see. Maybe someone taking what's not really their's. A now and then, "kick in the door" tantrum! Hell to pay! A trip to the principal's office!

Moonlight Cruise

There was a Midnight Cruise advertised for one summer night in North Sydney harbour. The dialogue. Are you going? Who else is going? Can I go with you? We were all worked up about it, we girls. The night arrived. We were looking for an exciting and romantic evening. Being all of 15 years old at the time. Judy, Ethel, Joan B, Lorna, Fay, Joan P, Roberta and I got on the boat. Not that many others with us. That was a bit disappointing. No interesting boys to speak of! The water was as calm as calm could be. We hadn't even started out when suddenly a voice yells out, asking, if anyone has a "Gravol". It was Fay. I couldn't believe what I was hearing. There wasn't even a ripple and we hadn't left the dock! Lorna happened to have a bottle of "Gravol" with her. She gave one to Fay and then Fay told us she couldn't swallow it. She tried and tried. It was the tiniest pill you ever saw in your life! We all burst out laughing. We couldn't believe it! We went on the cruise without Fay taking the pill. We circled the harbour and back again. That was it! No romance, whatsoever. That was our Moonlight Cruise!! The most exciting part of the whole thing was the pill. Fay didn't get seasick!!

Swoon Time

Peeking through the lace curtains trying not to be noticed. I am all ready to be picked up for a date. Cars going by, but not the right colour. Waiting and wondering if he is going to show up? I keep looking! Did he forget? Did I get the time mixed up? Is he with someone else? Checking out my reflection in the mirror. Doing it again! Getting fidgety!! I finally see his car coming and I am feeling very relieved. The doorbell rings. I am jittery and giddy! There is no mention to him that I have been in a "panic". I am very cool about it all. Out we go to the car, lickety split. He opens the car door for me. I'm sitting in the front seat. He climbs in, shuts the door and puts his left arm through the open window. Both of us, a little bit nervous! We take off with the radio blaring. In no time at all, I am sitting in the middle of the seat. Ever so slowly, his right arm is around my shoulder. Swoon time!

The Pit Stop

I have a thing about clean windshields. One afternoon, Judy has the car. I happen to say that the window is very dirty. Maybe saying it more than once! She just ignores me and we keep on driving. Before long, I ask Judy to stop at a gas station so that I can use the bathroom. There was no problem about our stopping. I do my "dirty deed". When I get back in the car she keeps saying, "It's clean, it's clean." Very excited about it and all! She's pointing and pointing. I finally notice she is talking about the windshield. "Clean as a whistle." She said, she told the guy at the garage that her MOTHER wanted clean windows. Meaning me! Was I embarrassed? The guy looking at me and all. Not at all!

Back of the Class

What's there to be doing in a boring English class! You're tired of looking out the window and shuffling in your seat. Thumbing through your textbook. What topic to be writing on for your essay? Bob Patey,

Jackie Gallop and I play x's and o's and hangman to relieve the monotony. We make a point of sitting at the back of the classroom, each class. Maybe, Mrs. Blane not really noticing us. The fun we have passing the hangman paper, back and forth. A circle for the head, dotting the eyes one by one, the nose and then the mouth goes in. A line for the neck, the body, two for the arms and legs. The dashes we put down for the word or words we think up, on the bottom of it. Guessing the letters and the hangman hopefully not filled in. Our minds in two places at once, as we might be asked a question as we are playing. Not knowing what the teacher asked! Mrs. Blane never catches us! Is it fun!!

Cruising

"Cruising" downtown on a Friday and Saturday night. Driving along tooting the horn at almost every car that passes. We know most of our friends parent's cars by sight, seeing them so often. We are all out looking for a good time. It isn't unusual, for us kids to be hanging out the car windows and yelling at each other. So much fun doing it! Messed up hair in the breeze and lots of giggling going on. Kids yelling at each other where to meet or you might change cars and drive off with someone else. Maybe, a dance going on at the high school or meeting up at one of the hamburger shops, later on. I saw Donnie "cruising" one Saturday afternoon, stopped by the traffic. He was looking and admiring his reflection in "Moore's Electric" store window. He was driving his yellow Pontiac convertible. Did he think he was hot!

Fashion Pieces

Reversible skirts are a must have if you can afford to buy one. They are $25.00 each. Very expensive for us girls. The skirts come in blue and brown tartan. Light blue, dark blue. Dark brown, light brown. Can you dance wearing one of them? They enhance your figure. Everyone is envious if you are wearing one. They all have to touch it. Do they twirl when you are dancing! Such a great look at skating. A cashmere twin set completes the look. Tartan skirts with a horse pin are popular, too. Wearing a tartan flower sweater pin. A black sheath dress, straight skirts with a slit. Pea jackets and white bucks, saddle shoes and bobby socks. Pennies for your loafers. You are cool, if you have any of these items. Our mothers stitch up the legs of our strides and our jeans to make them tighter. It's quite a job getting your feet through the bottoms of them. Some of the girls have poodle skirts and cinch belts that make your waist look smaller. Wearing nylons, instead of lyle stockings, is a real plus. Looking very grown up!

Pool Room Boys

The boys use Brylcream on their hair for the slicked back, greasy look. Complete with ducktails. The Elvis look! Some of the boys, think it is a cool thing, to go to the poolroom on Commercial Street. They like to play pool and snooker. That is their grown up thing to do. The smoke is billowing out the door from the cigarettes that are smoked. You can hardly see through the windows, they are all gummed up. The really cool guys put their cigarette packs in their T-shirt sleeves. Just like Marlon Brando. No girls are allowed to enter the door! We catch a glimpse as we pass.

The Mounties

On the way home, one Friday night, Kathy's Dad's car runs out of gas in front of the Mountie Station in Upper North Sydney. We girls are all in a flutter! Midnight being curfew time and all and we are way past it! No gas station around. Pitch black. No houses, anywhere around, to be seen. We all knew that we were going to be in the doghouse, when we got home. We had no choice, but to go up to the RCMP door and ask if we can use their telephone. After a few knocks, we can hear somebody coming. We are scared to death they might arrest us for being out so late! The door opens and there stands a Mountie in his long johns. Another one behind him in his long johns, too. They were in bed asleep.

We could hardly hold back the laughing. They looked so comical! Janet called her Dad and he brought us out some gas. We got home alright in the end. Our parents not too upset about our being late, when they knew the whole story.

Crazy 8's

Sitting around the kitchen table playing Crazy 8's. Going crazy yourself in the process. Eight cards each, the deck in place, one turned up. Following suits. The fun playing a Jack and having someone miss their turn. Pick up two cards, four, six, and eight with the deuces. The power you feel having an eight in your hand. Frustration when you get the Queen of Spades and you have to pick up five extra cards. Cards accumulating and accumulating, falling out of your hands. Slowly getting rid of them and getting them back again. Trying your best to get out first. No cards left in your hand! Oh's and darn it's and I don't want to play anymore. Or "I'm Out!" Hurray!

North Sydney Folks

Annie Phalen, Ronnie Green, Jimmy Harris, Margaret Prosser, Jan Stephens, Lois MacDonald, Jackie Gallop, Roy LeMoine, Joyce Sibley, Marcella Voutier, Margot Youden, Gloria Rose, Sid Hatcher, Georgie Moore, Dennis Almon, Crawford Hull, Eric Sibley, Garland Lillie, Marilyn Orrell, Marion Galpin, Clarence May, Joan Salter, Roberta Belmore, Joan Bond, Lila Camp, David Moore, Rhodina MacKinnon. Donna Palmer, Bomber Andrea, Dolores Bungay, Bobby Gray, Buddy Andrea, Gloria Lillie, Jackie Ford, Madelyn Lillie, George Camp, Bobby Blane, David Moore, Frances Turner, John Camp, Dougie Poole, Shirley Banfield, Marion Whittle, Margaret Anderson, Art Jackson, Johnny Meers, Verna Grandy, Shirley Grandy, Mabel Lemoine, HarrietStubbert, Kenny MacIsaac, Norma May, Roy Stoodley, Bob Standing, Jackie Gallop, Ethel Snow, Bob Patey, Bobby Cluett, Evelyn Rooke, Billy Youden, Lorraine Youden, Adrienne Angel, Mary MacLeod, Jackie Timbury, Winnie Bungay, Scott MacGregor, Earl Luffman, Peter Miller,

Sadie Walsh, Dexter Butt, Charlotte Reid, Vivian Malanka, Deanie Youden, Jackie Jesty, Carol Bond, Mary Lawless, Donnie Blane, Betty Hillier, Janet Thompson, The two Ducks from Sydney Mines, Jimmie Ivey, GRACE BANFIELD, Stan Gooding, Bruce MacLeod, Evelyn Burt, Travis Budge, Lila Bungay, Libby Brown, Teddy Brown, Jimmy Meaney, Ronnie Eavis, Marilyn Hare, Keith McNeil, Billy Moores, Keith Moores, Carol Edmunds, Ed Lawless, Thelma Meaney, Georgina Edmunds, Aubrey Clark, Terry Jackman, Clyde Garnier, Donna Crothier, Kenzie Kelly, Jane Crofton, Lynette Walters, Sharon Higgins, Gerry Lawless, John Clark, Gail Squires, Georgie Buffet, Danny Jesty, Marie Bond,John Orrell, George McNeil, Lois Jesty, June Stewart, Billy Shadforth, Sandra Shadforth, June Groves, Austen Grant, Marilyn Woodfine, Gwen Crofton, John Ivey, Sheila Scott, Harriet Stroud, Jean MacDonald, Billy Meany, Shirley Burt, Carol Shadforth, Huey Lawley, Camilla Farrell, Patsy Kenna, Jimmie Edmunds, Tina Collier, Sammy Farrell, The Banfield Girls, Marilyn Deyoung, Annabel Blagdon, Jean Martell, Isabel Lawley, Mildred Crewe, John House, Clayton Riggs, Crawford Hull, Donnie Boutlier, Georgie Buffett, Harriet Stubbert, Sonny Bungay, Art Hawkins, Gerald Crewe, Isabel Blagdon, Adelin Young, Marlene Stewart, Evelyn Burt, Vic Jenkins, Don Benoit, Doris Millard, Thelma Hatcher, Wendell Musgrave, Walter Jackson, Mildred Vickers, Betty Dearing, The Kinslow Girls, Charlie Blagdon, Clint Guy, Kilby MacClafferty, Monica Burke, Lloyd Burke, Tyra Jesty, Francis Quinn, Howie Collins, Alice Hawkins, Art Palmer, Sharon Higgins.

The Stars

Dennis Day, Jackie Gleason, Errol Flynn, Art Linkletter, Barbara Stanywick, Zsa Zsa Gabor, George Sanders, William Holden, Joanne Woodward, Joe DiMaggio, Fred Astaire, The MacGuire Sisters, June Allyson, Eddie Fisher, Lana Turner, Artie Shaw, Louis Armstrong, Dinah Shore, Donald O'Connor, Frankie Laine, Montgomery Clift, George Raft, Gene Tierney, Kim Novak, Jayne Mansfield, Paul Newman, Dan Dailey, Van Hefflin, Hedda Hopper, Pier Angeli, Dick Powell, Deborah

Kerr, Shelley Winters, Charlie Chaplin, Cary Grant, Gregory Peck, Charles Boyer, Audie Murphy, Judy Garland, Mickey Rooney, Howard Keele, Jane Powell, Margaret Leighton, Joanne Dru, The Everly Brothers, Chuck Berry, Bill Haley and the Comets, Ritchie Valens, Gene Vincent, Roy Orbison, Johnny Cash, Carl Perkins, Dick Clark, The Crickets, Alan Freed, Frankie Lymon, Jimmie Rodgers, Jack Scott, Little Richard, Catherine MacKinnon, Gordon Lightfoot, John Alan Cameron, Gene MacLellan, Bill Langstroth, Stan Rogers, Anne Murray, Rita MacNeil, Bruce Gouthro, ELVIS, Bobby Darin, Fats Domino, Tommy Edwards, Marilyn Monroe, Jane Russell, Tab Hunter, Troy Donahue, Rosalind Russell, Angela Lansbury, Joanne Woodward, JOHNNY DEPP!!, Ronald Reagan, Jane Wyman, Mary Martin, Shelley Winters, Elizabeth Taylor, Debbie Reynolds, Richard Burton, Richard Harris, Pier Angeli, Vic Damone, Sammy Davis Jr., Doris Day, Frank Sinatra, Janet Leigh, Red Skelton, Charles Laughton, Bobby Darin, Donald Sutherland, Maureen O'Sullivan, Ann Blyth, Noel Coward, Ruby Keeler, Douglas Fairbanks, Jr., Vincent Price, Julian Lennon, Liza Minnelli, "Bonnie Raitt, Gladys Knight and the Pips", and Andre Bocelli.

Where is Smoky?

Smoky is my mother's cat. She is grey and white and a bit heavy. My mother likes to give her playful spankings. My mother became very sick and had to go into the hospital. Mum was in and out for quite some time. Smoky would sleep on her bed all day long. She left oil stains on the bedspread from her fur. My mother died. There's no describing your feelings. It wasn't a good time for any of us. Smoky seemed to sense that something had happened too. She would just mope around. Not very playful. A year later, we moved to Halifax to my father's new church. There were so many mixed feelings about our going. Leaving our mother behind and our friends. We couldn't find Smoky when we were setting out. Rev. Turner said he would get someone to bring her to Halifax. Two weeks later, Smoky arrived. We kept her inside getting her used to the house. One morning, Smoky went out and didn't come back. We looked everywhere. Everyone was so upset. As time passed, we gave up but still wondered. About five months later, Dad had a call from Rev. Turner saying that Smoky was sitting on the front steps of the rectory. In North Sydney! He said she was fine but very thin. A church couple brought her back again. She wasn't as lively as before. She wasn't looking too good either, her fur all matted. We kept her in the house again and let her out once more. That was the very last time we saw her. Could she have been in search of our mother?

The Fire

It was a very sad day when the parish hall and the church burned down, one January day. We had moved to Halifax a few months earlier. I was so relieved I wasn't there to see it! Everything gone! People crying. Disbelieving! The worst thing that ever could have happened! No one ever getting over it. A new church and parish hall now standing. They are just not the same as the familiar black buildings that stood so stately. I will never forget the fun times we had in both the church and the hall, and the quiet times. The physical memories gone.

Cape Breton Calls Me Home

Twenty five years ago I flew to Halifax for my cousin Janet's wedding. I had a week's holiday. My friend, Georgie, called me soon after I arrived. She wanted me to come to Port Hawkesbury for a visit with her. I suggested she come to Halifax instead. Georgie was my neighbour when I lived in Port Hawkesbury in the 70's. She drove to Halifax two days later. She "strongly" suggested we go back to Port Hawkesbury, visiting friends. I went along reluctantly because time was so short. We had a wonderful time taking in the church fashion show and playing bridge. The next morning, I was ready to leave for Halifax. Georgie insisted that it would be a shame not to visit my friends in North Sydney. North Sydney being so close by. She wouldn't let up about it. I kept insisting, I didn't have the time. There was no reason to go home to North Sydney. It was October. My friends who moved away came back in July and August. There was no point. My old gang not being there. I had to get back to Halifax for goodbyes. To family and friends there.

I soon found myself on the new highway in Georgie's very long, black Buick New Yorker. I am on my way to North Sydney! Just me in this very large car. Her credit card on hand for emergencies. When I spot the Wycogomagh road sign, I hear a terrible noise. It sounds like the bottom has dropped out of the car. Here I am sitting! No garage around. Everything so still and quiet. The Bras D'or Lakes in eye view on my right. A beautiful sight. Sitting and wondering what am I doing HERE!? Feeling very frustrated with my plight. A tow truck approaches about half an hour later. Relieved and thankful, I wave to him. He yells, "I will be right back." After several hours at the garage, I am on the road again. Sixty dollars lighter on Georgie's credit card. Problem solved. Here I am driving and thinking what am I doing? Realizing all of the time that has been wasted. Strongly realizing that I should be on my way back to Halifax.

At suppertime, I am driving up the very familiar King Street. My favourite, favourite, street. The black frame church and parish hall gone. I make the left turn on Pierce. I notice several men working on the rectory windows. I pull over and ask if they are renovating the house. One man yells out that the house is being torn down in the morning. I couldn't believe what I was hearing! What they said was such a shock and very upsetting. It was the last thing I ever thought could be happening! The home I shared with my family going to be gone as well as the church and the hall. My stomach sank. I got out of the car and I am met by two men from the church, who know me. Mr. Carter, the policeman, was one of the men, and Mr. Moore. They tell me a new rectory is going to be built on the same spot. I go in and walk through the house for a final look, for old time's sake. Room by room, I slowly go through. At snail pace.

A very sentimental time, a sad time, and a happy time. Lots of remembering going on in my head. I look out on the maple trees, more stately now, from Shirley's window. Our private place. It is such a still time. Solemn! I spend the night with Judy's parents across the street. In the morning, standing on their veranda, we all watch my house being bulldozed. Tears are flowing. I was so thankful that the Clark's were there with me. So fitting, their being my second family and all of us together. A big part of me disappearing before my eyes.

It was as if something brought me back for a final look. The physical memories all gone. Our good times in the house and in the front and backyard. The verandas, the staircases. Memories of my mother and the silly times. Mum hooking clothespins on the back of my grandfather's pants and his not knowing! Dad working in his study and on the telephone. Arthur, Shirley and me jumping up and down on the chesterfield! Throwing the cushions on the floor. Sliding down the bannister! Lined up for the bathroom! Watching television. Our meals together in the kitchen and the dining room. So many special times. The many people who visited us there.

All these years later, Georgie, still doesn't know why she kept insisting that I go to North Sydney. Preordained? I say that it was! I know I was meant to be there at that time.

The Lingo

Jelly rolls, fruit cups, tea biscuits, cocoa, margeen, coloured sugar, Hound Dog, Que Sera Sera, Rags to Riches, foot stools, wooden tree stands, "Elvis the Pelvis." skipping stones, "Sleepy Hollow," Mel Tillis, THE BEATLE INVASION, scarves, pedal pushers, penny loafers, brown suede jackets, paint sets, box socials, kerosene lamps, "Santa" and his sleigh, "Chances Are," hard balls, "Blue Christmas," colouring, fear of spiders, no mugs, hide and seek, FRIDAY THE 13TH, Giant MacAskill's shoe print? "Leprosy," Tea for Two," class clown, skipping school, "Bonanza," "Danny Boy," broken windows, Kilby, Easter eggs, "The Toast of the Town," burning schoolhouse, "Gone with the Wind," cash registers, cry baby, "We'll Sing in the Sunshine," white wall tires, tandem bikes, cowboy boots, date squares, "Tom Sawyer," pansy, washing your own car, smoke filled rooms, 5 cent phone booths, a boy opening the door for the girl, too shy to get up and dance, "Lady Chatterley's Lover," no jeans at school, cow manure, cactus, marching bands, "I'm All Shook Up," "Reggie Van Gleason," push lawn mowers, globe of the world, "one little piggie," "sticks and stones may break my bones," macaroni and cheese, three on a match, "Sugartime," "Eversharps," "Oxydol," bottle caps, tripping, treasure hunts, "The Tennessee Waltz," late for school, reef knots, kettles, car clutch, "Sunlight" soap, "Sixteen Tons," a penny for your thoughts, Robert Browning, "When You Walk Through A Storm, Keep Your Head Up High," taking a stroll, Sonny James, ketchup, typewriters, ear plugs, "The Mayor Of Casterbridge," turnips, nerves of steel, "Volare," gum drops, zylophones, yellow belly, shredded wheat, slush, note paper, want to go for a spin? having a hairy fit, a close shave, whiskers, scribblers, "That's Amore," being squished, "Coca Cola," memorizing the Nova Scotia Counties, empty pockets, adults only, taking it all in stride, private school, higgledy-piggledy, blond streaks, taking the scenic route, power play, a puddle jumper, the early birds gets the worm, fuddle duddle, wooden shoes, "Mona Lisa," Are you taking me for a sucker? Marshall Dillon, pencil cases, I bet you a zillion dollars, "Your Cheating Heart," I'll chance it, "How Much Is That Doggie In The Window," tire chains, "Honky Tonk Man," "The Titanic," black telephones, heads or tails, bad dreams, having a good time, "Little Red Riding Hood," a piece of gum, "7up," "Jeepers Creepers," "Gillette" razors, stop bugging me, Leslie Caron, "Mighty Mouse," pyjama bags, "The Three Little Pigs," "Whipper" Billy Watson, liar, liar, pants on fire, "Sunnyside of the Street," "Come Outta My House," "Jambalaya," "Coronation Street," getting the dirt, boys walking on the outside, hot rods, "There Goes My Everything," flag poles, "Sargent Bilko," the eye of a needle, I'm a wreck, my son, a wiggle and a walk, taking a leak, going all the way, knocked up, up the creek, really cool, "Bye, Bye Love," she's a hard case, "One day At A Time, Sweet Jesus," Nelson Eddy, light as a feather, jaw breakers, nail polish remover, holding your breath, bankrupt, "Lois Lane," Christopher Reeves, on your mark, get set, go, "Newfie Screech," checkers "I've Got You Under My Skin," shoe shines, "Picnic," lighthouses, "If God Brings You To It, He Will Bring You Through It," "Peter Pan", salons, coral, starfish, trophies, dog paddle, "Singer" sewing machines, moonshine, swimming at George's River, 52 pick up, girls and boys going to confession, a roll in the hay, manure, "Paper Mate" pens, fifty cent pieces, as slow as cold molasses, "Gigi," having your freedom, he's an old geezer, going parking, you old fart, don't bug me, everyone and their dog was there, get off my case, dead meat, "I Enjoy Being A Girl," "Quaker Oats," gum drops, cool cat, chop suey, ship shape, "Anchors Away," "Auld Lang Syne," Canadian Girls In Training, a quickie, son of a gun, "Searchin," the little dipper, "Lassie," drop earrings, 562 Squadron, see you later, alligator, I can't see you for looking! everyone and their dog was there, "La Bomba," "String of Pearls," "In The Mood," Brenda Lee, Wayne Newton, "Whole Lot of Shakin Going On," big penny, splinters, wait till you get a load of this, weeping willows, kewpie dolls, fish pond, monkeys on a stick, popcorn, "Cupid," SAM COOKE, "The Andrew Sisters," "Boogie Woogie," "Bugle Boy," "Our God Is Marching On," "That's kosher," hip, hip, hurray, "Stormy Weather," Lent, stilts, "See The Pyramids Along The Nile," "m'm good," that's what Campbell's soups are" "The Golden Gloves," as the crow flies, tom cat, ice boxes, cotton candy, cross eyed, swiveling hips, call me, "Give Me That Rock And Roll Music," cameo pictures, doing the dip, brainstorm, onyx rings, "Jolly Green Giant," going to Maine, stamp album, stys, straight from the horse's mouth, evening bags, long sleeved gloves, knowing where the action is, "It's My Party," Leslie Gore, "String Of Pearls," double jointed, pinking shears, "Tumbling Tumble Weeds," fly off the handle, dirty hands, knock kneed, safety in numbers, "Pillow Talk," "Born Free," leapfrog, get the show on the road, she's a heartbreaker, spinning a yarn, "I Surrender," "Turkey Lurkey," "Ding, Dong, Dell," parcel carriers, "Going To The Chapel," mind your own beeswax, "Donner and Blitzen," ring around the rosie, chenille bedspreads, ship in a bottle, Fats Waller, I've got a handle on it, clothes whisks, powder puffs, "Share The Wealth," men's shoe rubbers, "Georgie Porgie," fireplace pokers, "Oh What a Beautiful Morning," nothing could be further from the truth, Saint's alive! "I Met My Little Bright Eyed Doll," "Hancock's Half Hour," maroon and gold,, hula hoops, never the twain shall meet, mahogany furniture, "Jimmy Crack Corn," southpaw, sour puss, leaving a tip, red, white, and blue striped balls, poker, Mickey Spillane, "Gorgeous George," seeing your reflection, the devil made me do it, match sticks, having your own compass, printing in the lines, Clint Eastwood, "Spellers," I couldn't see it for looking, half dead, 99 and 44/100 percent pure, card tricks, "There's A Place For Us," playing the spoons, "The Rain in Spain," the world is coming to an end, today! Longitude and Latitude, "Jimmy Crack Corn," "The Itsy Bitsy Spider," chenille bathrobes. jawbreakers, "Dumbo," "Goo Goo's Gifts," a happy medium, MAUD LEWIS, "Sweet Caporals," robbing the cradle, "I Can See Clearly Now," "Buckley's Cough Medicine," "Wampole's Extract," Pottle's Lake, dice, wooden sleds, doll cut outs, fish cakes, your first watch, cod liver oil capsules, tooth aches, tying your own shoe laces, "Pot of Gold," "The Royal Family," men smoking pipes, ice cube trays, hot dogs, loco, cracking gum, rocking chairs, TV's in cabinets, vegetable peelers, life saver books, dates with icing inside, candles, using your father's razor, "Dragnet," 45's & 78's, Art Carney, teasing, skates, blocks, angel hair, playing cards, kerosene lamps, bugle boy, book worms, elastic bands and rolled up pieces of paper, DIANA, stuck up, cracking your knuckles, down in the dumps, "Elmer Fudd," stringing you a line, a piece of cake, not a stitch to wear, CAPE BRETON ISLAND, wanting to go steady, Mitzi Gaynor, "Old Maid," having a hairy fit, none of your business, bathroom scales, in a pickle, paper folding, "Galway Bay," "Cry Me A River," cuddling, "I'm Gonna Wash That Man Right Out of My Hair," a ricer for potatoes, coloring, getting your licence, dictionary, "Alley Oop," "Freshie," Tom and Jerry, stick 'em up, "Going down Memory Lane," 98 pound weakling, "Elsie," the cow, the smell of gasoline, Diana Lynn, Vera Lynn, Gracie Fields, "Movin' On," "Mule Train," "On The Wings Of A Dove," spitballs, your shoes in mud puddles, squishy! Kick the can, "Robinson Caruso," "Bless This House," "I Heard It through the Grapevine."

Not living in the real world, a mind of her own, tomorrow is another day, don't burn the house down, with bells on, don't blow a gasket, let's get this show on the road, Princess Elizabeth and Prince Philip, you had better watch your step, you don't quit, as fit as a fiddle, fooling around, "It's Raining, It's Pouring," putting on the dog, "Don't Let The Sun Catch You Crying," such goings on, up your nose with a rubber hose, chew the fat, a friend in need is a friend indeed, "Howdy Doody," "she has a lot on her plate," "what a thrill," conceited, stuck up, I creamed it, "Yellow Bird," the breakups and back together agains! "Rain, Rain Go Away," Trigger, "The Wonderful World of Disney," very true, The Wysocki Family, clothes inside out, "I Love You A Bushel And A Peck," "here is the church, here is the steeple," knee high to a grasshopper, "Dagwood," coconuts, rain dance, coal stoves, "Everything Is Beautiful," Fatty and Skinny, tracing, she's hot and cold, "Home Sweet Home," "The Academy Awards," "Bugs Bunny," bows and arrows, mustard plasters, "Calamity Jane," two left feet, no talking in church, look for the silver lining, "They Called It Puppy Love," "Return to Sender," Don't press your luck, "Climb Every Mountain," zoom, zoom, crows, fainting in church, A'hem, stay where you're at, I'll come where you to, A fine piece of stock, "Blondie," "Our Miss Brooks," Richard Crenna, Betty Hutton, Cornell Wilde.

"How Many Arms Have Held You"? "Heidi and Peter," "Have You Ever Been Lonely"? Maurice Chevalier, rootin' tootin', buckles, flattery will get you nowhere, being struck by lightning, "The Royal Wedding," it's no joke, "When You're Smiling," puppy love, mouth organs, comical sticks, "he's a crock," "Could I Have This Dance For The Rest of My Life?" "Walking The Floor Over You," lots of gumption, "Freddie Fender," "Lonely Teardrops" candelabra, cattle herds, player pianos, pins and needles, glooscap, rhythm, "Are You Lonesome Tonight," "Harbor Lights," I can't find it for looking, "It's A Long Way To Tipperary," stealing a base, right on the tip of my tongue, moving and grooving, what breed are you? The Lordie Thundering, catching your breath, "Only Love Can Break a Heart," blush instead of makeup, ("I have sinned! It was terrific!"), "making a spectacle of yourself," she served a purpose, "Summertime Blues,," sunburns, "Star Light, Star Bright," "Yankee Doodle," watch your step, joe blow, putting on the Ritz, "Wrap Up Your Troubles," hobo, "Fly Me To The Moon," clickety clack, in a fog, icicles, if I had my way, "The Milky Way," up on a pedestal, piddling, "The United Nations," hurry up!, "Fibber Magee and Mollie," Chuck Berry, fleur de lis, "God Save The Queen," a piece of cake, Rhythm & Blues, "Killarney," she's doing a number, "Oh Darling," my pet peeve, kick the can, "A Hot Time In The Old Town Tonight," the CBC, Dr. Jekyll, "The Lullaby of Broadway," bloody murder, Duke Ellington, Glenn Miller, Artie Shaw, Benny Goodman, "I Could Have Danced All Night," "Shakespeare," follow the leader, foolscap, a peeping tom, "Green Acres," the gospel truth, the Cavalry, putting on the dog, "Buttons And Bows," "good things come to those who wait!," I'm going great guns, CJCB, "The Farmer In The Dell," "The Queen Elizabeth's Coronation," Brenda Lee, golly gee, Morgan Fudge, great scot, gee whiz, Ed Asner, let's get this show on the road, going berserk, driving me up the wall, Doris MacGregor, rain dance, man's best friend, STELLA, flip a coin, Sam Medjuck, go bananas, "Candid Camera," say cheese, Karl Malden, skeletons in your closet, burned down to the quick, Blackett's Lake, "Masonic Lodge," synagogue, Ethel Mertz, Fred, all thumbs, sweet dreams, Johnny Carson,

"The National Anthem," pack up your troubles, Jack Lemmon, the girl next door, Arthur Godfrey, a pie in the face, wet paint, Dr. David House, merci beaucoup, Eddie Albert, "Money For Nothing," don't have a conniption fit, don't have a hernia, twisty, Wayne Newton, "The Diamonds," hands up, "et tu, Brutus," sour puss, "Georgie Porgie," admiring your reflection, "Ain't That A Shame," "Yes, It's Me, And I'm In Love Again," "I'm Walking"- to New Orleans, "Blue Monday," "poor Me," FATS DOMINO! the devil made me do it, Eva Marie Saint, Richard Kiley, Ed McMann, match sticks, Alan Arkin, having your own compass, Eddy Murphy, 007, I couldn't see it for looking, Zena Sorge, your dreams coming true, Joe Namath, transistor radios, walkmans, "Westinghouse," "Massey Ferguson," "Let's Here For the Boy," gas powered lawn mowers, half dead, "Henny Penny," "Chinese Checkers," Your Cape Breton accent suddenly returning when you are "down home" for a day, smarty pants, "Rollover, Beethoven," the tango, "Only the Lonely, "Anne of Green Gables," Audrey Meadows, Steve Allen, Victor Mature, Hedy Le Marr, Bob Hope, Bing Crosby, "On The Waterfront," Eva Gabor, Eileen Brennan, Irene Ryan, Jennifer Jones, Tennessee Ernie Ford. "How Great Thou Art," "Shall We gather At the River"? Cliff Richard, "The Great Escape," Ryder rental truck, "Ocean's Eleven," "The Mummy," "Frankie and Johnny," "Cheaper By The Dozen," "The Stepford Wives," "No One Hears But Him," "The Cat in the Hat," "The Wild One," "Dracula," "Heart Light," "Godsend," Harry Chapin, Mary Strickland, Gilbert and Sullivan, "Mortimer Snerd," flower power, "Laugh In," "The Fire Dwellers," Hugh Garner, Margaret Laurence, electric lawn mowers, PETER WOOD, $20.00 bills with the devil in the Queen's hair, recalled, "Aerosmith," "My Big Fat Greek Wedding," "I Walk The Line," "Last Dance Last Chance," "Simon and Garfunkel," "The Manchurian Candidate," "Alice Doesn't Live Here Anymore," "Constant Craving," isn't that a corker?, "Angelina Cacciatore Spaghetti And Meatballs," "Disney World," always mindful of the needs of others, black clothes, a sign of mourning, "Easter Bunny," "Rag Mop," "Moonstruck," "Here Comes That Rainy Day Feeling Again," leaving things up to chance, "the didoes," "Trace Pace," going from strength to strength, Harold Ramsay, DISCO, Mike Douglas, "Liz and Dick," shrinks, "Piglet," "Green Eggs and Ham," "Curious George," "The Jetsons," "Natasha," "Bullwinkle," "Spaghetti Westerns," Walt Disney, "The Haunted Mansion," "The Orient Express," "Dirty Dancing," "The Good, The Bad and the Ugly," "Up The Down Staircase," "Sailor Moon," "24," Sandy Dennis, Sylvester Stallone, "The French Connection," "The Karate Kid," "The Planet of the Apes," "The Three Musketeers," Fred Gould, BILL WOLK, chocolate covered bananas, John Parsons, "Times Tables," stale potato chips, "ON BROADWAY," homemade play dough, beer bread, "SALLY," "The Rotund One," "Frank's Band Stand," "The Public Gardens," Frank Reid, taking vitamins, Charles Kuralt, "The Mutiny On The Bounty," "Last Tango In Paris," "ALL THAT JAZZ," "When You Only Got 100 Years To Live," "Imagine," peace talks, "The Black Donnelley's," "WACO," Keanu Reeves, FLORA, "COLUMBINE," "OKLAHOMA BOMBING," using your imagination, a time for dreaming, find a penny, pick it up, TWINKLE AND BUNNY, electric fans, "BOND," "JAMES BOND," "Laugh IN," Reuben Cluett, Anne and Don, "Summer Breeze Makes Me Feel Fine," "The Statler Brothers," Fred Waring and his Orchestra, "Diana Ross," Jimmy Dean, "The Andy Williams Show," Brian Donlevy, "Needles And Pins," BON JOVI, "SONNY AND CHER," "The Beat Goes On"! "I GOT YOU BABE,"

"Half Breed," "Sitting On the Dock of the Bay," "Lazy Days Of Summer."

Richard Thomas, "The Beverley Hillbillies," "Cheers," Joan Rivers, "As the World Turns," "Three's Company," "The Waltons," "Finding Nemo," no pets, no smoking, no bare feet, no drinking! "Swiss Chalet," "Red Lobster," recycling, "please wait to be seated," chili peppers, "Car 54, Where are You"? "The Young and the Restless," "The Hunt For Red October," Kevin Costner, "The English Patient," Bruce Willis, Cybil Shepherd, "The Secret Storm," "General Hospital," "Search For Tomorrow," "Coronation Street," "Sixty Minutes," "ULI," "The Jack Paar Show" EDNA THOMAS, Johnny Carson, "WKRP in Cincinnati," The Manchurian Candidate!, John Diefenbaker, FLORA

MACDONALD, "Martin Luther King," Billy Ray Cyrus, "Barbie and Ken," "Judge Judy," Rene Levesque, "The Maple leaf Forever!" deadheads, "The Guiding Light," "Soap," pumpkins, "Forever Plaid," Randy Travis, Ruth Hatton, "My Baby Loves The Western Movies," a "senior moment" "Get Ready," "spirits," USSR, digs, "Larry KingLive," Basin Street, "Yuk Yuk's," "My Mother the Car," Ronnie James, ARIFAT!! the slow posties, subway, Neil Armstrong, look alikes, stop lights, Bette Curtis Connolly, "The Milk Calendar," "Lucy In The Sky," "That's Why They Call It The Blues," empty pockets! L'Oréal, "It's A Sign Of·The Times," beauty salons, iced tea, "Scooby Do," 15 minutes of fame, corn chips, visit us online, MYRTLE AND LORNE HOWARD, wading pools, "Biography," credit cards, H20, bathroom pit stops, "The Wonderful John Kay"(Politician Extraordinaire) "Four Hands and Two Pianos," Brian Tobin, "Venturers," Janis Booth, being in great pain and bearing it as best you can, "True Courage," Louise May Alcott, "Sleepless In Seattle," "All Systems Go"!, "There Goes My Everything," Kiefer Sutherland, "Harry Met Sally," GARY AND STEPHANIE! "See You in September," Christopher Reeves, "Fahrenheit 9/11," "SILVER CROSS" losing your life for your country!! Being shipped over seas, "Secret Window," Jane Lockwood, inground pools, John Dunne, dishwashers, "Big Yellow Taxi," Tony Danza, Angelina Jolie, best sellers, 5 pin bowling, "We'll Sing In The Sunshine," the devil made me do it, short and sweet, going batty! going to camp, John Voight, joggers, THE BOOTHS, THE HEASELL"S, cutting the grass, BLT's, the soaps, dog and cat carriers, "Park and Fly," warm ups, rentals and sales, house and garden tours, "Bingo," "Come Back Little Sheba," "Hazel," Hepatitis C, "Seniors" Recreation Centers!, "Hagar the Horrible," cruises, rain forests, newspapers galore, "As The World Turns," "Saturday Night Live," "The Lion King," "SCTV," "Three's Company," "Annie," "Peanuts," Charles Schultz, "Legally Blonde," "Urban Cowboy," "Absolute Power," "Put Up A Parking Lot," George Hamilton, "Cosmopolitan," "Cracked Magazine," "Starsky and Hutch," polls, "Pickles," "Spiderman," "The Big Chill," "Field Of Dreams," "Brian's Song," "Evita," Kevin Bacon, convertibles!, "There's

Something About Mary," Peter Kormos, Alexa McDonaugh, "Mystic River," "Bye Bye Love," Reba McIntyre, "Saturday Night and I Just Got Paid," Dwight Yokum, Roger Miller, "Hollywood Squares," Bob Barker, Mr. and Mrs. Ed Mirvish, JOHN DENVER, James Caan, Conway Twitty, Alan Bates, Lionel Ritchie, Michael Caine, Al Pacino, Joe Pesce, "Suspicious Minds," Frank Panabaker, "Come On Down," Georgie Matheson MacDonald, Dennis James, coffee shops!!! take out!, "When I Was Seventeen," Sherry Wysocki, Larry Blyden, Greg Kinear, Jack Nicholson, Robert De Niro, Sean O'Sullivan, Joyce Cooke, digital camera, air conditioning, Tony Blair, RUTH TRIPP AND MELINDA, "Glory, Glory, Hallelujah," Sir Winston Churchill, cell phones, "The Walls of Jericho," laptop computers, "The Buchta Dancers," John "Q". Holmes, Joe Watkins, sports writer, Gary Wilson, Nancy Waye Lawrence, "Bits and Pieces," Bill Lawrence, "Tiny Talent Time", CBC News, ALLISON, TRACEY AND ANGELA, has your

money been counted out at the check out counter? Ann and Gord Elop, "King of the Road," Hugh Grant, Connie Smye, moccasins, peace pipe, "Neeva," Shirley Booth, Hugh Hefner, Princess Diana and Prince Charles, Dr. Barbara Holmes, panty hose, "Strangers In The Night," smokers/non smokers! loonies, "How are your inners working?," you can drink as much beer and wine as you like--, Nelson Mandella, Bishop Desmond Tutu, Marg Osbourne, Charlie Chamberlain, Martin Luther King Jr., "HISTORIC CHURCHES" DISAPPEARING!! Jewellery collections, Connie and Bob Smye, "Monday, Monday," (Your cat and dog's reaction to a vet! Do they have any choice about going??), bottled water!! Bowel obstructions! take out, strip malls, box stores, lost in the subway system, condos!!!, turn it up!, marijuana bars?!, "Shopsy's," karaoke, Jean Charest, "Cape Breton Clubs" "Noah and the Ark," "The Royal Canadian Legion," "THE DROWSY CHAPERONE," "MOMMA MIA," Jessica Walters, Denny Doherty, "Little Old Lady From Pasadena," Blanche Dubois, Clint Eastwood, John Cassavetes, Gina Rowlands, Ted Knight, Valerie Harper, walking under a ladder, Goldenrod, Timothy Bottoms, "Little Darlin," "Wolfman Jack," Joseph Bottoms, "Sunshine On My Shoulders," Shirley Meade, Michael

Douglas, Edna Thomas, Burt Reynolds, Gary Conway, Donna and Larry Webber, Don Messer, "ZIGGY," Jeff Bridges, Nick Nolte, John Travolta, line dancing, Donna Summer, "Last Dance, Last Chance For Love," Dusty Springfield, "Black Cars Look Better In The Shade," Tracy Chapman, "Dire Straits," "You Don't Have To Say You Love Me," John and Elsa Lee, "Amazing Grace," Julian Lennon, Jeff Healey, "Dear Abby," Santana, bee and wasp stings, poison ivy, Ruth, how can you do that, man? "Just For You," blue bath tubs!, Jacob's Ladder "Come Back To The Five And Dime," "Kentucky Rain," reading your comics under the covers with your flashlight, Bobby Jackman, "Good Morning StarShine," Karen and Darcy Want, Jessica Tandy, Hume Cronin, "JAILHOUSE ROCK," "CATHY" the comic strip, "I Want You, I Need You, I Love You," whistling, "It's Now Or Never," "Flying On Your Own," "A Reason To Believe," "I'm Mr. Blue," Rusty Springfield, "You're 16, You're Beautiful, And You're Mine," "SEASONS OF THE SUN," Peter Frampton, "Venus," "Don't Let The Sun Catch You Crying," "Walk Right In, Sit Right Down," "Every Day."

A boy Named Sue, "You Are There," "The Green Door," purse strings, sly as a fox, deer crossing, butterscotch taffy, "Acadian Bus Lines," "Heaven, I'm in Heaven," x marks the spot, puffed wheat, "The Plouffe Family," "Freddie the Freeloader," eye patches, mittens on strings, "Gomer Pyle," Jim Nabors, arrowroot cookies, fun seekers, "Sweet Marie's," a dirty deal, good luck charms, tom foolery, "Henry Aldrich," where is your mailman? you're a coward, dogs without leashes," "I, Calypso," people sitting on verandas and front steps, biting your tongue, having your own goldfish, hair set, Easter lilies, guns and caps, street hockey, Ker plunk, a letter to the North Pole, dare, Jessica Best, double dare, hats with veils or feathers, "Great Balls of Fire," Bobby Darin, hide and seek, Rob Dezoete and Jade, boobs, piddling, "Twenty Questions," "The British Kept Coming," memorizing, (animal, vegetable or mineral),"5 foot 2, eyes of blue," "Charlie Brown," step on it, if looks could kill, keeping your fingers crossed, what a drip, pucker up, stringing someone along, "The Lord Of The Dance," this will drop your socks, quick as a wink, "A Band of Gold," polka dot bikini, digging for clams,

"Who Wrote The Book Of Love," she has a heart of gold, "The $64,000 Question," "Playboy," a puddle jumper "I'm Just A Lonely Boy," Amber, Jason and Cloe, VERA, Shamir, the early bird gets the worm, fuddle duddle, wooden shoes, Agatha Christie, "Do You Want A Dance?" are you taking me for a sucker?, pencil cases, Woody Woodpecker, "I Never Felt More Like Singing The Blues," fizz, nose drops, Art Carney, Jackie Gleason, "This Diamond Ring," Charlie Rich, "Thelma and Louise," "Mutiny On The Bounty," "Don Juan De Marco," Stan Rogers, Eartha Kitt, Ella Fitzgerald, THE MAKKEY FAMILY, "Big Girls Don't Cry," "Cherie, Baby," "The Four Seasons," Oscar Peterson, "The Locomotion," "Cape Breton Passports"! "I Will Follow Him," "Lies," "Farewell to Nova Scotia," "Snow Bird," John Allen Cameron, up town, down town! That's some good, The Dee Family, "Robbie Lane and the Disciples," "Timber, Miss Jess, Winston, "Raffy, Martha, "Jessie," "Max," "Roxie," "Heidi," "Spooky," "Where Can My Baby be?" Amy Johnson, Jeanne and Edwin Slack, "Archie," You haven't got a leg to stand on, "High on a Mountain of Love," the final leg of the journey, "Alice Blue Gown," tardy, "Rule Britannia," fog, minding your p's and q's, Methodists, undertakers, families looking after their loved ones at home! "Jasper," cartoon, "WHERE'S THE BEEF," "IODE," "Allied Youth," Mr. Lawley, garden parties, "Billy Boy" pedal organs, Bowden's Jewellers, Cowboy Copas, Heinz ketchup, "SCOTTIE POTATO CHIPS!" tastes good like a cigarette should," tripod music stand, "For Once In My Life," cool guys, pony tails, "The William Carson," arborite tables, lots of "old" back roads, Marlborough's, men's and boy's short haircuts, dinosaurs, "Have You Got Cheating on your Mind," Ray Johnson, "THE SALVATION ARMY," I'm A Believer," meeting your Waterloo," corsets, "A Whole Lot of Loving For You," good things come to those who wait, don't beat yourself out! "Our House Is A Very Nice House," "Orange Lodge," MIKE and HELEN, Pastor Perry Rockwood, Don Gibson, Mary Scott, the holy rollers, Frank's Snack Bar, Union Jacks lining the streets on Dominion Day, "The Gospel Hour," Billy Graham, "JUST AS I AM," you are gone in the head, "Earth Angel," Oral Roberts, you can't change him, many happy returns, Rex Humbard,

ROGER WHITTAKER, Buster Keaton, Tibbs, Grant and Al, Provincial Exams, It's not how you look on the outside, it's how you look on the inside! "Davis Cup Winner"- (Peggy Day), ("Schoolboy Curling Champions")- Billy Youden, Paul Reid, Paul Rice, Allen Kenny, (Union Jack flags, Princess Elizabeth's pictures in every classroom), "The Lord's Prayer" being said in class, dried out cod fish, fish and brewis, what if they turned you down? "Patience and Prudence," "To Know Him is to Love Him," "It's 11:00 pm! Do you know where your children are?" blackand white television sets, Valda Vooght, "springtime melts the snow," "If You've Got the Money Honey," "The Cisco Kid," Mitzi Gaynor, Eh? Let sleeping dogs lie, Johnny B. Good, Chet Atkins, "Nearer My God To Thee," when you're hot, you're hot, Johnny Rivers, "Stupid Cupid," "Kentucky Woman," FM Radio, "that nice man on the radio," Don Parrish, Bob Soulsby, FRANK MAGAZINE, "The Three Tenors," The Ecumenical Movement, "When A Man Loves A Woman," "Where Can My Baby Be?" KENT, AL AND CAROL, "E Mails," Luther Vandross, Barry White, Puslinch, Kona, Hawaii, Don Ho, having good friends, keeping in touch with family, "RESPECT," "Lazy Crazy Days Of Summer," "She's a Day Tripper," go west, young man, "Snow White and the Seven Dwarfs," "Just One Look," Donald and Ivana Trump," "Let It Be Me," "Baby, I Need Your Loving," "Rosalie," "She's Come Undone," "Blood, Sweat and Tears," "I Can't Get No Satisfaction," "Let Me Tell you About The Birds And The Bees," "Silhouettes on the Shade," HARRY CHAPIN, "Hey, It's Good To Be Back Home Again."

"Seinfeld," Dorothy Kilgallen, Bobby Curtola, John Daly, Ethel Mertz, Tommy Hunter, Tommy Common, Charlie Clemens, cold as an icicle, "Your Hit Parade," hand jiving, Yes, "Jesus Loves Me," "Benny and Joon," Honda CRX, lotteries, B&B's, second hand shops, weight loss clinics, "Boardwalk,"" Me and Bobby Magee," "The Old Spaghetti Factory," "Ginsberg and Wong," Paul Newman / race car driver, ROBERT REDFORD, lube change, NICOLE SIMPSON, RON SILVER, "Cecilia," "Dream Lover," "It isn't nice to fool Mother Nature," electric razors, Ken Maynard, B.B. King, bridge mixture, squeal on someone, "Mule Skinner Blues," Littlest Hobo, friggin', Bon Ami,

'Ben's Bread"/ two for fifteen cents, "Yesterday," "Hey Jude," Sheriff's posse, Glen Ford, cheers, "The Irish Rovers," "Cabbagetown," Sandra Dee, MacDonald Carey, "Garfield," Charlie Rich, escape the summer heat, "Edward Scissorhands," "Big Apple," drowning in debt, 5 day weather forecast, "Dynasty," health care crises, Emails, "People Magazine," "The Osmonds," "In My Room," video games, 8 tracks, Candace Bergen, floods, DNA! flashbacks, "The Pirates of the Caribbean," "terrorism," TAXES, "Beverly Hills," 90210, "The Way We Were," Audrey Hepburn, granola, fast foods, "Halston," "Liz Clairborne," cosmetic surgery, Mary Ann Shuett, "I Am Woman," Frankie Valley, "The Commodores," "Murder, She Wrote," cassettes, "Solitary Man," "A Kind of Hush," "The Dave Clark Five," Terry Cooke, (OMOD) videos, CD's DVD's, "Moosehead" beer, Kris Kristofferson, Dudley Moore, RONNIE HAWKINS, coupons, rain checks, Christian Dior, Randy Bachmann, "Hi, how are you today?" "THE BEACH BOYS", KENT STATE, JEREMY, DIANE, SUZANNE, TIFFANY

(Tiffie Shade) ADRIENNE, NOAH, hippies, looking out for #1, golden oldies, color tv's ASHLEY MACISSAC, "Canadian 3000," omens, Dead, cool!, "She's Come Undone," "THE NICKEL NEWS," forever young, "The Simpsons," beatniks, double, double, "Bachmann, Turner, Overdrive," "The Doobie Brothers," BERKLEY, "oldies but goodies," top 40!, "My Favourite Things," Holly Golightly, cheesies, AM Radio, VIRGINIA CAMERON,(WV) flower children, "Fleetwood Mac," "Let It Ride," Fidel Castro, "These Eyes," "American Women," the year 2000, Bette Midler, "The Doors," "Taking Care Of Business," "Bo Weevil," "Strangers In The Night," REINIE VAN RAATH, MICHELLE DUGUID, MARCIE GUITAR, DENNY DOHERTY, NORMA

ELLIOTT, "The Whole Cameron Clan," "Mary Poppins," "Crispy Crunch," "Wonderbar," Bar BQ's, "If You Can't Stand The Heat, Get Out Of The Kitchen," Lover's Lane, heroes, Bill and Betty Philips, lemonade stand, cops and robbers, showgirls, GARY HARBER, see the world today in your Chevrolet, sharks, family heirlooms, vroom, vroom!, ARCHIBLA! Gypsies, "Ol' Man River" thunder and lightning, "Anne

Landers," Laurie, Lauren and Sean, "Show Boat," psoriasis, rheumatism, Natalie MacMaster, hoop crinolines, "Silhouettes On The Shade," ribbon, cowboy hats, ½ price sale, sombreros, Brian, Annie, don't strain your eyes, don't forget to turn off the light, big shot, Queen Victoria, "Hurricane Hazel," world tours, black tie!, AUNTIE SHIRL, A line dresses, men's briefs, royal crowns, "Dancing the Night Away," kangaroos, "What In The World's Come Over You,". pussy footing, night clubs, "It's Magic," astronomy, Happy Birthday, best girlfriends, It's nice to come back to the place where I was born, DAVID BAREFOOT, Stewart Cameron, CAROL ANN LEE, Sports, "Jerry Lee," dumb waiters, "Dion and the Belmonts," "The Wayward Wind," Gail Storm, "Ivory Tower," Dean Martin, beachgoers, calendar girls, decisions, decisions, "Canada Customs"!!, conflicts, dangerous drivers, Lydia and George, being on the defensive, Alice Lee, on common ground, casting your ballot, MARCIE BRILL, coffee breaks, Mathematics, coming out like a rose, people abreast of you, Ed Ames, Al Martino, The Drifters, "Smoke Gets In Your Eyes," "Shebib's Barber Shop," amazing! Bridge Tournaments, chess, ABBY CLAIRE, MADDIE, ELLEN, AMELIA JANE, (putting on a pretend show) DAVID/ fencing champ! Lingerie, Fabian, STEVEN TRUSCOTT!! (Innocent!) Can't see for looking, "DONUT CITY,""BRASS RUBBINGS," Barbara Hamilton, Eskasoni, "The Cat's In The Cradle," reach for the moon, The Jenkins, Arthur and Jean Williams, Wayne "G," The Fred Farrell's, "Herman's Hermits, "Bridget Loves Bernie," "48 Hours," "Down And Out in Beverley Hills," Cape Fear, Nick NOLTE, "What's Up, Tiger Lillie? (SUZANNE, thank you!) Vincent Price, Dr. Kenneth MacGregor, Glen Campbell.

Made in Japan, "Diana," real turtles from Stedman's, "Books of Knowledge," spruce beer, convertibles, Ralph King, polka dots, hooks & eyes, glue, "ROCK AND ROLL," "There's A Hole In My Bucket," "Who's Sorry Now?" penniless, "Maidenform," "Only You," flashing a moon, wake up call, Groucho, combination lock, "Velveeta," "Blue Moon," two pairs, lick on tattoos, "Star Light, Star Bright," "The Old Woman In The Shoe," Ricky Nelson, nine lives, Peggy Lee, sand pails, "WESTERNS," tinsel, "Somebody Loves Me," nothing to write home about, "Hokey Pokey," "Paula," straw hats, hiccups, "To Tell The Truth," Alan King, reading the menu, Harry Truman, vamoose, "Everything Is Beautiful," snakes and ladders, tiddly winks, NHL games, Yogi Berra, flat as a pancake, Liza Minelli, winking, "Hot Diggity," a wiggle and a walk, tripping over your feet, "Rambling Rose," tires without tubes, circumferences, drawing on your hand, "Glow Worm," "He loves me, he loves me not," "Jersey milk" bars, stevedores, "Red Rose Tea," how are you doin? Darlin, snowman, theorems, "You Are There," "The Greatest Show On Earth," Nole Pole, "Only You," A wiggle and a walk, fortune cookies, "I Believe," "Ozzie and Harriet," Kate Smith, Mahalia Jackson, Sophie Tucker, Alan King, George Harrison, "IF I CAN DREAM," Elvis!

"I'd Like To Get To Know You," "Here's To You Mrs. Robinson," "Poor Little Fool," Mel Tillis, "Peter, Paul and Mary," "Hang Down Your Head Tom Dooley," "I Will Send All Of My Loving To You," "I'm Mr. Lonely," Patti La Belle, Sweet Caroline," "Runaround Sue," "Help Me Information," "Poetry In Motion," "The Four Tops," "Nothing Can Ever Change My Love," "Born To Be Wild," "We've Got A Groovy Kind Of Love," "These Boots Are Made For Walking," "Surf City," "Won't You Stay Just A Little Bit Longer," Hey There, Lonely Girl," "My Good Luck Charm," "Monster Mash," "Up On The Roof," "Heat Wave," "Games People Play," "California Dreamin," "California Girls," "Breaking Up Is Hard To Do," "Over And Over Again," "I'm A Travelling Man," "Wake up, Little Susie," "My Candy Girl," Calendar Girl," "Duke Of Earl," "Johnny Angel," "My Way," "YOU SEND ME," "Air Supply," "Gonna Find Her," "Be My Baby," "I'm Crazy, "Let's Do The Twist," "My Baby Done Wrote Me A Letter," "The Beatles," "Do I Love You," Paul Anka, "She's Having My Baby," "Shylo," "Where Oh Where, Can My Baby Be," "Soldier Boy," "It's A Sign Of The Times," "Only Fools Rush In," "Sea Cruise," "Could You Ever Love Me Again?, "Get Back," "THE BEATLES!" "You've Lost That Lovin' Feelin'," "My Guy," "Walk Hand In Hand With Me," "Angel Eyes," "Break It To Them Gently," "I Don't Remember What Day It Was," "Sweet City Woman," "I Hear A Symphony," "What The World Needs Now," "The Winds

Of Life," "There's A Kind Of Hush," "Love, Love, Love," "Come On Baby Light My Fire," "ROCKY MOUNTAIN HIGH," "ANNIE'S SONG," "I'm LEAVING ON A JET PLANE," JOHN DENVER!!!, "Hotel

California," "The Eagles," "Earth, Wind and Fire," GAS for 29 cents a GALLON!!!

Tina Turner, "The Supremes," Gary Crosby, Mac Davis, JOHNNY DEPP, Gregory Peck, David Brinkley, John Glenn, "The White House" TONY SKARICA, Peter Lawford, George Carlin, Ricky Nelson, Tracey Nelson, Walter Cronkite, Jerry Van Dyke, Carol Burnett, Twiggy, Marianne Faithful, "The Rolling Stones," "Mr. Dressup," Cliff MacKay ("Holiday Ranch") Clint Eastwood, Ashley Judd, Dionne Warwick, Whitney Houston, "Raindrops Keep Falling on my Head," Burton Cummings, "Teenage Head," Arthur Miller, "McArthur Park," Steven Fuller, fiddler, James Hewer, artist, "Love Will Keep Us Together," Margaret Laurence, "The Green, Green Grass Of Home," Taylor Caldwell, Lindsey Wagner, Farah Fawcett, ANNE RULE (True Crime Writer), "The Pink Panther, "A Reason To Believe," Robert Downey Jr., Michael Bolton, "Grease," King Biscuit Boy, Kenny Rogers, Diana Ross, Stevie Wonder, MARIA, WILF, MONICA AND JASON, Ray Charles, MAE AND JOEY, ADA ROMANO, John Davidson, "The Fifth Dimension," "Hair," Tony Orlando and Dawn, Elton John, Eric Clapton, Carol King, Neil Diamond, Neil Young, John Lennon, "The Pointer Sisters," "The Beatles," 'THE SECOND DEBUT', Angie Dickensen, Harvey Korman, Patricia MacKinnon, Wynona Judd, Lily Tomlin, Jute Johnson, "Maude," "Archie Bunker," "THE CAROL BURNETT SHOW," Gary Moore, Alan Ludden, LEROY PEACH and Barbara, "PEACHTREE PUBLISHING," Tim Conway, Marianne, Peggy Cass, "Cheers," Vicki Lawrence, Lyle Waggoner, "The Stampeders," "Sandler and Young," Mac Davis, Kitty Carlisle, Durwood Kirby, Haygood Hardy, "The Goodtime Hour," Bobby Vinton, The Pink Ladies, Frenchie, Stockard Channing! RITA MACNEIL, GORDON LIGHTFOOT, "Lucille," Aristotle Onassis, "The Kennedys," Ed Asner, Mary Richards, Rose Marie, Mort Sahl, Dick Van Dyke, Morley

Amsterdam, Carl Reiner, Laurence Harvey, Nicholas Cage, Cher, "Flying On Your Own," Carly Simon, Bill Langstroth, Paul Anka, Tom Cruise, Natalie Cole, Tammy Wynette, Aretha Franklin, "The Blues Brothers," Nana Mouskouri, Barry Manilow, James Taylor, "Pretty Woman," Natalie Cole, Darryl Hall & John Oates, Rod Stewart, Boy George, Dan Ackroyd, Kenny Loggins, Shania Twain, "Snow Bird," Loretta Lynn, Dolly Parton, Jane Fonda, Johnny Cash, Julian Lennon, ASHLEY MCISSAC!, Phil Collins, Patsy Cline, "CREEDENCE CLEARWATER REVIVAL,"

Celine Dion, Bruce Gouthro, Carly Simon, Ike and Tina Turner, "The Guess Who," Footloose, JOE COCKER, Del Shannon, "Island Girl," "The Wonderful Wizard of Oz," Don't Go Breaking My Heart," "CANDLE IN THE WIND". "It's Now Or Never," Keep your shirt on, there's no place like home, sugar cones, snowmen, ringlets, buttercups, "Cabot Trail," burning school houses, grasshoppers, "Blue Boy," "Old MacDonald Had a Farm," blabbermouth, blowing bubbles, evening purses, "Dragnet," "Kellogg's," slipping on a banana peel, a telegram, birthday suit, the end of the world, going for a spin, chicklets, raising the roof, outhouse, wool sewing cards, "Treasure Island," no rhyme nor reason, telling a fib, fig newtons, poop deck, French safes, a tell-tale sign, glory be, Jesus Murphy, hi doll, runs in your nylons, "Juliette," clutch purses, plucked eyebrows, "SHIRRIF'S," "You're a Slowpoke," brush rollers, trick or treat, bib aprons, scarves, twin beds, I'm a Little Tea Pot," hair nets, "Autumn Leaves," half-slips, popsicles, Frigidaires, polka dots, nylons with seams, "Borg" jackets, men's handkerchiefs, fur muffs, "God Save The King," chalk dust, "Zippo" lighters, billboards, your first puff, peachy keen, summer days, rugby, boy's white socks, rushing to class, jeans, a phony, school bell, powder room, identification bracelets, stuffed poodles, eat your heart out, photo albums, perfumed letters, head bands, making out in the back seat, "Pontiacs," hip, cripes, high heeled shoes, "At The Hop," "Tears On My Pillow," have a ball, "The Blob," Jerry Lewis and Dean Martin, Studebakers, "Edsels," fudgsicles, sun dresses, lollipops, she's off her rocker, ankle bracelets, "The Mummy," JOHN CANDY "Canadian Bacon," "SIMON BIRCH," MARLON!!

"Wait now," hot and bothered, making out, View masters, cracks in the sidewalk, horsing around, ain't that the truth? freckles, "Jack and the Beanstalk," ribbon candy, merry go rounds, naturally curly hair, "Pinocchio," burn rubber, an apple a day, "pin the tail on the donkey," clockwise, go fish, zing go the strings of my heart, we snuck in, red light/green light, stepping down hard on the gas, bailing, school time, amethysts, promenade, apple peelings, seagulls, a story at every street corner, rowing a dory, Hank Snow, shift on the wheel, sleeping over, licking the bowl and beaters, she's a wreck, eat my dust, pickup truck, baby doll pajamas, no mailmen, lord it all over you, "Purple People Eater," they're from the country, Hydramatic cars.

Kleenex, "go team go," Korean War, hula hoops, going home for lunch, "Kotex", free admission, "Cracker Jacks," a walk down memory lane, out to lunch, "Players," please, put some meat on your bones, 1,2,3, Alera, look for the silver lining, I have to get my beauty sleep, spanning wrists, red cross pins, "Buttermilk Sky," writing in a straight line, a penny for your thoughts, time marches on, "World Atlas," badminton, birdies with real feathers, this is the "Operator," number please, "The Grand Old Duke of York," tight as a drum, footloose and fancy free, silver dollars, "did you hear the latest?"

Ferry rides, squinting, quick as a wink, baby blue eyes, god love ya, "pretty maids all in a row," two bits, got a smoke, Frank Sinatra, cherry cokes, Humpty Dumpty, tooth picks, "East Side Kids," Ovaltine, flat as a pancake, how can Santa come with no snow on the ground, Abbott & Costello, broken windows, a feather in her cap, "Winchester Cathedral," playing in the creek, photo corners, snow flakes, winking, Topo Gigo," It's In The Book," biting your tongue, stubbed toe, 'Libby's" beans, bossy, wetting the bed, sweaters with angora collars, cream puffs, homemade mitts and gloves, a light over your left shoulder to read, Leo Dorsey, Girl Guides planting bulbs beside the creek, bean suppers, candle light dinners, Easter baskets, jelly beans, vanilla cokes, "An Inspiration Lady," "SUNDOWN," Doctor Barbara Holmes RN, Jennifer, Laura, Melody Lee, Andrew and Olivia.

Mickey Mouse, "Elephant Walk," clean as a whistle, bone dry,

"Singing in the Rain," he's robbing the cradle, "Long, long ago," "The Three Stooges," shoplifting at Stedmans, rabbit stew, "Home on the Range," Merry Christmas To You, cream on top of milk, leather gloves, apple jelly, stewed rhubarb, corned beef and cabbage, spankings, tooth powder, bread and molasses, ear muffs, fox stoles, eggnog, snap, card shufflers, nursery rhymes, train sets, paper snowflakes, boxes of stars

,(red, silver and gold), St. Pierre, Miquelon, pantry, clothes pegs, sharing a cigarette, speeding, icicles, bullshit, licorice all sorts, the catechism, second gear, afraid of flunking, "Englishtown Ferry," she's got steam heat, t shirts, clip on sunglasses, brooches, hot dogs, bobby sox, candles, hammocks, I wouldn't be caught dead going there, radio, no veterinarians, the boogeyman, shuffling your feet, blowing your own horn, making pompoms, sticking to you guns, corking, cut-outs, stamp and coin collections, dictation books, making the rounds, square dancing, Tommy

Edwards, cute, sneakers, peanut brittle, yodeling, bats and balls, "Shuffling off to Buffalo," umbrellas, wooden window screens, pulling taffy, petit fours, musical chairs, tootsie rolls, pucker up, knee high to a grasshopper, Camel cigarettes, crewcut, in a snit, snakes and ladders, hairnets, 45 player, "Spam," tooth fairy, parking meters, twinkle twinkle, car sick, "High Noon," cat's cradle, "Park Place," "Coca Cola," a wiggle and a walk, lipstick on your collar, "Music, Music, Music," wooden nickels, "Fifth Avenue," "Broadway and 42nd Street," cream puffs, chocolate éclairs, "Lipstick on Your Collar," Connie Francis, Buddy Ebsen, Max Baer, Sally Struthers, Gloria Swanson, Jean Stapleton, Carroll O'Connor, Louis Armstrong, William and Harry, Arm wrestling, 4 eyes, crew cuts, hair parts, men smoking pipes, Kodak camera, stamp collecting, coin collecting, chasing butterflies, looking for 4 leaf clovers, catching grasshoppers, riddles, biggest bubble without it popping, Jughead, ear muffs, blowing off dandelion fluff, ant hills, school pictures, wild strawberries, Lizzie Borden, ink stamps, collecting leaves, spruce gum, break your mother's back, stars on good papers, the end of the earth, whistling with grass, fly paper, running out of gas, fear of failing, Heinz 57, dictionary, eye glasses at Stedman's, blabbermouth, whispering in class, cuddling, V neck sweaters, pedal pushers, sneakers, cod liver oil pills, Swanson TV Dinners, TV trays, Hire's orange crush and rootbeer.

Put a penny in the parking meter, put a nickel if you're going to stay late, can't you read it says violation and if you don't pay you'll see the magistrate.

My old flivver is a good old friend. All you have to give her is a twist and a bend. She ain't worth a nickel but I bet by gee, she brought a million dollars worth of smiles to me. She needs new tires front and rear, the horn won't speak to the steering gear, she's a little lopsided and the lamps won't light, but outside of that my flivver's alright. Honk diddly honk honk, beep beep.

Thompson High School Song

Thompson High marches on with banners flying high Maroon and gold we know will never, never die Sportsmanship, games and play, we're always on the top Good old Thompson will never, never stop.

As we march along, singing our song, our spirits always high All the other schools we'll always cheer for you

For together we will have many good games But always to old Thompson we'll be true.

Written by Joan Bond

Cheering for Thompson High. Friends, Judy (second from left), partial Allie Jean (far right)

Acknowledgement

MY THANKS TO ANDY PHILLIPS, WHO HELPED ME SO MUCH TO GET THIS LITTLE NUMBER PRINTED. THE MOST LOGICAL AND CLEVERIST MAN I KNOW. I WILL ALWAYS BE GRATEFUL TO ANDY. A TRUE FRIEND!

I HOPE YOU ENJOYED THE BOOK AND READ IT MORE THAN ONCE.

AJH

Snapshots of Alice's Life

Alice looking "fab"

Very rich

(meet the mellers)

Choc Fudge

4 cups white sugar
1 2/3 cups evaporated milk
pinch salt
24 L marshmallows
1 cup butter

Boil on med heat in saucepan after it comes to a boil (and well blended) cook 5 mins more stirring all the time

Take off stove
add 12 ozs semi sweet choc. morsels
Stir til all melted and smooth

add 1 tsp vanilla
2 cups chopped walnuts (or your choice)

Grease 2 8" square pans
(let set til cool & set

Store in air tight cans

Dar said the name of the game

Delicious

TID BITS
From the Kitchen

COOKBOOK

YUK YUK
UP COMEDY

Excerpt from Alice's Codicil

I am so proud of my children and grandchildren, spouses. I love you all very much. It brings tears to my eyes!! Special kisses for all of you.

I feel I did my parenting well and this is being passed on to my grandchildren. Family and education are very important. Also caring for others. Dad and Grandmother Hodder stressed this. Putting yourself last.

Wishing you all a rich and rewarding life with much happiness. I love all the visiting that has been going on among you. The cousins and parents so close to each other.

My ashes will be buried in North Sydney along with my parents. An afternoon tea party I would like with a wine toast to me!!

I wish to acknowledge my very good friends of so many years standing. To be so blessed!!

Alice Hodder Hoyt,
July 2007

Excerpt from Alice's codicil and her signature

Alice's Eulogy by Allison

When I tell people my mom died they say they are sorry for my loss and then they ask how she died. When people hear that a middle-aged friend's mother has died it conjures up images of what they know to be a mother....someone who loved them, cared for them, looked after them when they were ill, took pride in their accomplishments, perhaps did a bit of baking and knitted some tea cloths. And my mom did all those things. But she was so much more than that. I'd like to tell you how she lived.

Anyone who knew my mom in the day would describe her as a fun, optimistic, very busy person. She raised four children, mostly on her own. She published a book about her early life called Judy and Me. She ran for council with a platform of affordable housing and services for teenagers in the town of Ancaster. She acted in plays, danced to her favourite music, visited friends, played the piano, boggle and bridge, shopped across the border without claiming her purchases ... and sometimes she did three or more of those things all in one day!! My mother was the person you could call at any time of the night with a problem (and she felt welcome to do the same which could be problematic at times). She was the family historian and knew the birthdates, anniversaries and death dates of all of her friends and family members.

Many of you know that my tiny mother was just 69 when she died. She had ten grandchildren whose photos and drawings were plastered over the walls of her apartment, who became known as "the beauties." She had a brother, sister, a nephew, four nieces, a nephew, two great nieces, a great nephew, lots of cousins and approximately 1000 friends.

Until a few years back, if you asked my mother her age, she would tell you that she was 16 in her head. In 1957 my mother turned 16 for the first time. In her book she recounted fun tales of dancing to the jukebox in the soda shop while wearing her poodle skirt... a cigarette in one hand and a milkshake in the other. She had an amazing memory for detail and could recite stories that no one else remembered. She had her driver's license, a backseat full of girls in poodle skirts in her father's car and the world by the tail. My sisters, brother and I could sing the lyrics to her high school theme song as she would often sing it to us. Those were the golden years.

The trip took a detour in 1961 after I was born. She and my father left Nova Scotia, her friends and the soda shop and made their lives in Ontario. At 28 years of age she had four kids underfoot. There was a lot of fun to be had in those days and some of our friends came along for the ride. A hand on the wheel of her car and the other hand holding a cigarette or swatting at us in the back seat, my mother would take us on daily adventures. She'd load us in the car and we'd do an activity called "dropping in on people." Here is how it went. Mom would toot her horn on the way up someone's driveway. This could be one of her close friends, a high school boyfriend, an ailing relative, or someone she knew of who lived in that particular town you were driving through. If it was meal time that was no problem, she probably had a bag of banana muffins in the car to share. We would all spill out of the car – perhaps with a dog or cat in tow. Then she'd have us kids do up the dishes and we'd be gone as fast as we came . . . tooting the horn on her way out of the driveway.

One of her friends told me that after a visit from my mom she plopped herself face down on her bed and didn't get up for eight hours!! Mom's visits were fun, but exhausting. She was always full of stories. For the most part SHE told the stories and you listened. She took us to lessons, concerts, the theatre, camping trips (sometimes she'd remember the tent poles), Florida vacations, and so much more.

My mom was very much a "my way or the highway" kind of person. You were to come along for the ride. She had no time for "moping around" and no time for sitting around. She'd tell you what you'd be doing and when. And that's what she'd call it … "doing." I recall a camping trip where we took my great aunt Elsie along to Nova Scotia. I don't think Elsie had ever been on a camping trip . . . and certainly not with my mother. Next thing you knew Elsie was spitting on an axe to sharpen the knife to cut the fruit for the breakfast we were hosting for the guys on the motorcycles camping in the next camp site. "We're doing Elsie!" she'd say.

After the grandchildren were born she and her dog Jessie would hop in her white Honda Civic and drive to visit them. Sometimes with an invitation, but sometimes as a surprise. She would have gifts with her for whatever occasion it was. If there was no occasion, the gifts were because she thought of you when she saw it. The gifts were thoughtful, usually inexpensive and could sometimes be somewhat unusual. "I got these Santa candles at the second hand store. Christmas is over so you can use them at Valentines' day as they are red." And if she visited you on Valentine's Day and weren't displaying them she would go into your cupboard and get them out for you. She, on the other hand, could re-gift what you gave her. She would give the sometimes quite expensive gift to someone she thought would love it even more than she did. And sometimes you'd never even heard of that person!

My mom had some faults. She didn't see them as faults and she did not wish to discuss them. She, on the other hand, was free to let you know your faults because that was called constructive criticism. My mom was a Taurus.... bull headed and proud of it. At any given time she had at least one person she was, quote, "on the outs with." Then she'd decide she was no longer on the outs with them and they were to apologize, or accept her apology, and move on. No moping about it.

The rules of life did not apply to my mother. She was charming and could get away with anything. She parked wherever she wanted.. She would call the fire department to take the dead mouse out of her sink as they had nothing else to do anyway as they were just playing cards. She'd flash the customs officer her baby blues, tell them she knew his mother in Nova Scotia and off she'd go, car full of undeclared purchases.

All the energy she expended would eventually catch up with her and she'd have to rest up...perhaps even check into the hospital for a time. She had suffered many losses, her parents, her dog, her driver's licence, some of her independence. The hospital visits would become more frequent. She'd tell us she would keep up the fight but, in my brother's words, her fun gas tank was empty. As her cousin Jean said, she lived her life backwards and had her golden years first.

After she surrendered her drivers' licence it was harder to drop in on people. The friends she had made in the building would pick up her groceries when they went to town. Some would pop over with extra chicken they had cooked for dinner. Charles would send his cat across the hall for a little visit. She would reciprocate and take them a little something (a couple of muffins she baked or a gift that you had given her). Her close friends would pop in and take her out for dinner or a drive in the country. They were doing for her what she had always done for everyone else. Mom didn't pop in anymore. We would pick her up and bring her to our homes to visit when she was well. It was harder for her to travel. She would email each of us or call and leave messages on our voice mail. She never used complete sentences: "played a little boggle today, ate yogurt and a banana, there was a pigeon on my balcony…it was your aunt's birthday today and your uncle's is tomorrow . . . hope all is well with you, call when you can, love you."

When we learned that my mom had died we needed some time to plan an event to pay tribute to her memory. We had to tell our children the sad news about their fun granny. We had protected them from the sad parts and they had only seen granny when she was "doing."

A few of the people in my mom's apartment building would tell me that the little lady in apartment 816 had been a special person to them. They didn't know the half of it. But they knew most of it.

A few of us were "on the outs" when mom died. Some of us called it needing a little space. We'd been along for countless rides and little did we know this would be the last. We had our families, jobs and other responsibilities to attend to as well, this year more than most. No regrets. Mom cherished all of her friends and family members. Mom would never have wanted anyone to look back with regret or guilt. Quite the contrary…oh no, oh no, not at all she would say.

As I read this I can envision my mother in the driver's seat of a red convertible. She's sixteen again. Elvis is in the passenger seat, departed friends, family and pets piled up in the rear. The tunes are blaring… mom's got a cigarette in one hand and is blowing kisses with the other. The fun tank is full and all is well.

Allison Blanche Hannah, July 2010

Alice and Me

I shall pass this way but once. Any good that I can do or any kindness I can show to any human being; let me do it now. Let me not defer nor neglect it, for I shall not pass this way again.

~ Etienne de Grellet (1773-1855) Quaker missionary

Crossing the Bar

Sunset and evening star And one clear call for me!
And may there be no moaning of the bar, When I put out to sea,
But such a tide as moving seems asleep, Too full for sound and foam,
When that which drew from out the boundless deep Turns again home.
Twilight and evening bell, And after that the dark!
And may there be no sadness of farewell, When I embark;
For though from out our bourne of Time and Place The flood may bear me far,
I hope to see my Pilot face to face When I have crossed the bar.
~ Lord Alfred Tennyson, 1889

Gaultois ferry, Newfoundland

About the Author

The author, Allie Jean Hodder (aka Alice Jean Hodder Hoyt Garland) (1941-2010), was a mom, granny, pet lover, letter writer, storyteller, health care aide and friend to many. Judy and Me was written when she was in her 60s, as a legacy to her friends and family.

Alice left her beloved North Sydney in 1958 and raised her family in Ontario. She considered Cape Breton her home and returned at every opportunity.

She died in Dundas, Ontario on July 26, 2010.

www.ingramcontent.com/pod-product-compliance
Lightning Source LLC
LaVergne TN
LVHW051005080826
845145LV00009B/2471

* 9 7 8 1 9 8 7 8 1 3 3 5 7 *